Scary to Tell the Woke in the Dark

The Tired Moderate

Welcome to my stupid brain.

Copyright © 2021 by Tired Moderate, LLC
All rights reserved. This book or any portion thereof may not be reproduced or used in any manner whatsoever without the express written permission of the publisher except for the use of brief quotations in a book review.

Printed in the United States of America

I'm supposed to leave this page blank for some reason. Seems kinda weird.

Table of Contents

The Terrifying..7

    No...8
    Thanksgiving..11
    Building a Better Tomorrow...................................15
    The Phone Call...20
    Pull the Plug...24
    Tuition ... of Death..29
    Algorithms for Algorithms.....................................33
    The Critic..37
    Judgment Day..41
    The Loneliness of Sainthood..................................43
    The Fugitive..45
    Zing!..49
    Fog of the Damned...52
    The Test..55
    High Beams...57
    The Big Sleep..59
    The Job Interview...61
    Erased...64
    The Hotel Room..66
    Moving Day...68
    When the Music's Over..71

The Whimsical...74

    Call Me Ishmael 75

New Cat, Same Cradle..76
Groundhog's Dinner..78
A Simple Matter of Measurement...............................80
The Unbreakable Bodice...82
Serenity Now..87
But I'm Not a Conservative!...90
Fight the Mustache...93
Ugly..96
A Thrilling Conclusion...100
Intro to Neo-Pronouns..103
Imagination..107
The Scorpion and the Frog, 2021..............................110
Must be Nice..111
The Sleepy Dog..113
The Superstition of Elders...115
Another Great Day..118
The First..120
The Balloon...123
A Simple Lesson...125
The Swinging Door..128

The Just Plain Weird...130

Assault on Jupiter..131
The Least Dangerous Game.......................................136
Critical Magic...142
The Hunt for Green October.....................................146
Life Support..149
Ascendancy..151
The Eagle, the Bear, and the Dragon........................154

Jeffrey's Pimple..156
Jeffrey's Pimple - Alternate Ending..........................158
Dear Johns...160

The Preview..163

The Author..166

The Terrifying

No

"No."

"What did he say?" asked Phillip.

"I'm not sure," said Mary. "It sounded like the first letter in the N-word, but followed by the 'O' sound. Do you think he's racist?"

Their confusion was mirrored by the rest of the first-year medical students, who hunted amongst themselves for one who understood this strange sound their professor had made.

"Maybe it was an autonomic response," offered one. "Try again."

Phillip cleared his throat. "Professor, the phrase you used is offensive. We demand an apology."

"No."

This was clearly no autonomic response. Phillip grew angry. "Sir, we *demand* you apologize now."

"No."

"We will report you," threatened Mary.

"No."

The students shared worried looks. None understood what was happening.

Phillip, being the sharpest of the bunch, adapted

first. Leaping to his feet, he stormed to the professor's desk and leaned across it. "We said apologize. *Now*."

The professor folded his short, thin arms across his chest and reclined in his chair. "No."

By now it was obvious that "no" meant the professor wasn't going to do what they'd asked, causing a litany of emotions to burst from the student body. Some were stunned to silence, while others quietly wept. A few grew furious, making all manner of threats to the professor's reputation, career - even safety.

But still he persisted.

Finally, Phillip calmed the room enough to enunciate his ace in the hole. Strolling back and forth between the professor and students, hands clasped behind his back and a pensive frown glued to his brow, he eventually sighed and spoke. "You're aware of the university policy on hate speech, professor. I'm afraid you leave us no choice." He whirled in dramatic fashion, raising an accusatory finger. "We're going to tell on you."

The professor snorted. His chest and shoulders jerked as he lost the battle to control his giggling.

"Stop it!" Phillip raised his fist. "I demand you stop, or I'll -"

"NO."

The class spun at the booming voice behind them. There stood the president of the university, flanked by dozens of old people. None appeared the slightest bit amused.

"No," repeated the university President.

A heady silence descended, until a shaky voice asked, "Mom? Dad? What are you doing here?"

A middle-aged couple stepped forward, their anger palpable throughout the room. "No!" both shouted. "No, no, no!"

The pattern repeated itself, parents of all races, sexes, religions, social status, educational backgrounds, and ages, forming a single, coherent voice.

As silence re-emerged, the professor stood. "Now, as I was saying, when treating a pregnant woman[1] …"

---

[1] Web Search: "medical school pregnant woman apologize"

Thanksgiving

Beth hated Thanksgiving. Every year she resigned herself to another round of family banter ranging from problematic to outright toxic. But this year, this year would be different.

"Everyone hold hands," her mother said after the family was seated, "we must say grace."

Beth's parents held hands. Her little sister across from her, her party-boy uncle, and her three surviving grandparents, they all held hands.

Just not with her.

She looked at her uncle to her left, her hand outstretched. She looked at her maternal grandmother, widowed by cancer two decades prior, on her right. Both held hands with their other neighbors, but not with her, choosing to place their free hand in their laps.

"Umm, hello?" She shook her hands at them. They ignored her. "Whatever, stupid superstition anyway."

Her mother finished saying grace, and the usual chaos erupted. Dishes were passed back and forth, silverware was freed from napkins to clatter across plates, laughter and light-hearted conversation bounced throughout the entire family.

Just not with her.

"Can I …" The gravy came and went in front of

her. She reached for the stuffing, only for her uncle to steal the serving spoon for himself. "What's with you people?" She finally cried.

No one answered.

"Hey," said her uncle. "How do you make five pounds of fat look good?"

"Oh boy," muttered her father.

"Put a nipple on it!"

Beth's mother slapped him across the head while laughing.

"You're serious?" asked Beth. "That level of fat phobia and body shaming is so 2005." No reaction. "Whatever."

"Did you guys catch that trailer for The Mandalorian?" asked her dad. "This is the first time I've been excited for a new Star Wars since Episode one …" The table shared a moment of silence.

Beth fumed.

"*You guys?*' Why would you think that's okay? More than half the table identifies as female."

"I don't know," said Beth's sister, "I miss Cara Dune. I can't believe they kicked her off the show."

"Are you kidding me right now?" shouted Beth. "Gina Carano hates trans people and made anti-semitic -"

"Right?" interrupted her grandfather. "People just

toss accusations around nowadays and we're all supposed to pretend we believe them."

Beth sat gaping at her grandfather. She expected some wrongheaded views out of any baby boomer, but to question the disruption of systemic racism by holding people accountable for their views was simply fascistic.

"She was such a badass," continued Beth's sister. "I wanted to be like that." She pecked at her food while her parents exchanged a concerned glance.

"This is so wrong," said Beth. "First of all, gender's nothing but a social construct designed to oppress women and benefit men. The only reality for *'women'* in a patriarchal society is their bodies are regulated by men. Men do whatever they want. They run the world! They own everything, they control everything. Gendered socialization is the reason there are so few 'badass women' in movies."

Beth's father placed a hand on her sister's shoulder. "Maybe it's time you tried a mixed-martial arts class." His eyes misted as he lifted his gaze to the ceiling. "Maybe that would have saved your sister."

"Honey no," said her mom, standing up to hug him from behind. "Don't punish yourself. Not today."

"We all feel it." Her grandmother wiped away a tear.

Beth sat in shocked silence. Were they talking about *her*? Why? How? SHE WASN'T DEAD!

"It was a mistake setting her place at the table,"

said her mom as she broke down. "I thought it would help. I thought it would honor her memory, or help us feel her presence, I don't know." She sobbed into her husband's back.

The rest of the table faced Beth, tears tumbling freely as they looked through her.

"What are you saying?" asked Beth. "I'm ... dead?" She felt her own eyes well up. "I'm not dead!" she shouted. "I'm right here! Mom! Dad! Grandma!" She knocked her chair over standing up, but no one reacted. She pounded the table. No one reacted. Finally, at wit's end, Beth turned and fled. Her fevered brain reminded her that ghosts could walk through walls, and, with a thunderous BOOM! she collided with the front door.

She was weeping now, in terror, in pain, in confusion. She flung the door open and ran.

Her family continued to weep for another minute before her grandfather stood up, walked to the front door, and shut it.

"Jesus Christ, I thought she'd never leave."

Building a Better Tomorrow

Artie was wired, but then, Artie was *always* wired. "Okay everybody, let's review. Step one: decide …" He stopped talking and pointed to a young woman in the front row.

"Um, what I want?"

"Yes! Awesome! Decide what you want. If you don't know where you're going, you'll never get there." He clapped his hands with a grin. "Step two: get …" This time he chose a young man near the center of the room.

"Lever … action? I forgot."

"Close. Leverage. Get leverage over yourself by associating pain with the negative habits you've formed over the years, and pleasure with the new, better habits that'll help you get …" He pointed to the young lady from step one.

"What I want."

"Exactly. Now step three is where we see some action. Where we interrupt …" He picked a young woman hiding in the back. She just shrugged and went back to dorking with her phone. Artie frowned at her, but his momentum pushed him onward. "The limiting pattern. We interrupt the limiting pattern."

"What if you're the limiting pattern?" asked a woman in the front row.

"You usually are," said Artie. "Without

understanding our true potential, we set artificial limits on -"

"No, not 'you,' like 'everybody,' *you* you. What if *you're* our limiting pattern?"

That threw Artie off his game, but he recovered quickly. "I don't know. In over twenty years of doing this, I've never been called a limiting pattern. Let's explore this. We've never met before today, right?" By the end of the question, he had his entire strategy mapped.

"We didn't have to. You're a white, male baby boomer in a suit. Do you have any *idea* the damage you've caused?"

Before he could blink, Artie's strategy evaporated. He leaned against the podium, and stopped moving for the first time in forty five minutes. "I'm sorry, I don't follow."

"You come in here telling us to dream big, like we all have your privilege. Do you know how upsetting this whole ordeal has been? I mean, look around. Half the people in here are women, and more than half are people of color."

"I'm lost. What does any of that have to do with setting and achieving goals?"

Someone across the room made a fart noise with their mouth. "Typical."

"What?" Artie faced the new voice.

"People of color are marked by race and inferiority

in the white mind," said a young man as he stood[2]. "The fact that you didn't even mention it ..." He dismissed Artie with a wave and sat down.

"Right?" said the first woman. "He comes in here telling us to 'visualize experiencing our goals,' when white people like him measure the value of their lives by the absence of people of color."

Several people began snapping their fingers.

"Okay," said Artie, "I don't know where all this is coming from, but I don't believe any of that. You're not inferior, and my life isn't better without you in it. Now, let's get back to realizing the goals we envision. Step four." Artie thought about calling on another audience member, but decided against it. "Create an empowering alternative. Don't wait for rock bottom. Look around now! What could you change today? Maybe it's something small, like," he smiled at the woman in the back row, "spending less time on your phone."

"Excuse me?" said the man next to the phone dorker, the latter having missed the dig. "Do you think it's funny punching down?"

"Punching ... what? Nevermind. Look, it was just a joke." Artie patted the air as he spoke, hoping no one else would aggressively derail his talk.

A white woman stood and faced her peers. "I'm so sorry everybody. We all have so much work to do, so much to learn. I know that anti-blackness is

---

[2] Every convoluted and stupid point in this scene is a direct quote from, or slight paraphrasing of, Robin DiAngelo. All the helpful parts come from Tony Robbins.

foundational to our very identities as white people." She shot Artie a nasty look. "We promise to listen. To do better."

Artie found himself speechless for the first time in decades of public speaking. "Anti-blackness," he finally sputtered. "What are you *talking* about? I'm here to *help black people*. And white people. And Asians, and Latinos."

"Latinx," someone shouted from the back.

"Shut up," snapped Artie. "Enough of whatever this is. I don't care about black people. I care about *people*. I don't care about white people. I care about *people*. I want your lives to be better. I've dedicated *my* life to making that a reality. But hey, if you don't want to work the program, if you want to spend this time yelling at me for having the wrong skin color, or being too old, I can't stop you. You need to decide if you want to build yourself up, or tear me down."

The audience fell silent, until a quiet sniffling drew everyone's attention.

"I'm so sorry," said a young man. "I promised myself I wouldn't cry, but the racial trauma I'm experiencing right now is too much." He fanned himself with one hand as the woman next to him wrapped him in a hug and glared at Artie.

The last ten minutes of his presentation were surreal, and he eventually stopped pushing back against the cries of white complicity, epistemological violence, and various forms of normativity. Rushing from the stage, he stopped in a nearby restroom to splash water on his face and get his bearings. With a deep sigh, he decided to call his wife and let her know what a bizarre day he'd had.

Forty six unread texts?

With some trepidation, Artie opened the first text he saw. It was from his business partner.

"I can't believe you'd say that. Do you have any idea what you've done? You're trending on social media right now. I'm sorry, I have to distance myself."

In a fugue state, he read the next message, this one from his sister.

"Wow, Artie. I never bought into your whole 'helping people' shtick, but wow."

His phone rang. He answered it. It was the CEO of the company he'd just given his presentation to. A man he'd known for more than a decade. Artie was fired.

Slumping against the nearest wall, he opened his social media. There he was, trending. Numb from the carnage of the previous five minutes, he scrolled down until he found a video of himself. It was a four second loop of him shouting at a crowd of young professionals.

"I don't care about black people. I don't care about black people. I don't care about black people."

The Phone Call

It was a dark and stormy night, and Edie needed popcorn. After all, a popcorn-less movie was hardly a movie at all.

Her head told her to keep things light hearted. With her parents gone for the weekend, she was alone with her cat, Baxter, and both frightened easily. But there was nothing fun about playing it safe, so she chose a slasher flick.

Curling up on the couch with Baxter, she hadn't finished the opening flashback to the killer's traumatic childhood, when her phone rang. Unknown caller. Though tempted to ignore the it, she answered, in case it was her parents using the hotel phone.

"Hello?"

"If you fulfill your obligations everyday you don't need to worry about the future."

Edie held the phone in front of her face and stared at it. "Excuse me?"

"It took untold generations to get you where you are. A little gratitude might be in order."

"Who is this?"

"If you're going to insist on bending the world to your way, you better have your reasons."

"I'm hanging up now."

Perturbed, Edie ended the call and soon forgot about it. The killer, after all, was stalking his teenage victims through a house just like hers, though they didn't know it yet. As the killer prepared his first ambush, the phone rang again.

Without thinking, she answered.

"Walk tall and gaze forthrightly ahead."

"Excuse me?"

"Dare to be dangerous. Encourage the serotonin to flow plentifully through the neural pathways desperate for its calming influence."

"I don't know who this is, but it isn't funny. Stop calling me."

She'd neglected to pause the movie, and having to rewind it to watch the initial kill again put her in a foul mood. So, when the phone rang a third time, she angrily smashed the "Ignore" button. Baxter stood and stretched, and Edie seized the moment to refresh her popcorn and soda.

The storm had grown to quite the tempest in the half hour she'd been absorbed in eighties camp, and repeated lightning strikes flashed outside her window as she pulled a fresh bag of popcorn from the microwave. The thunder was nearly instantaneous.

Slightly shaken, Edie returned to the divot she'd left in the couch. She suddenly felt grateful the couch was pressed directly against the living room wall, and wondered if it might be time to watch the episode of The View she'd recorded. There was speculation Joy Behar would do black face again.

The phone rang, interrupting her internal debate. Unknown number again. She hit Ignore. This time it rang immediately.

"Look, this isn't funny, and I'm not scared of you." She realized she was shouting.

"Compare yourself to who you were yesterday, not to who someone else is today."

An icy sensation stabbed its way through her torso. Slowly, carefully, she stood and studied her surroundings. "What did you say?"

"Perhaps you are overvaluing what you don't have and undervaluing what you do."

"If you call back I'm calling the police." She hung up and immediately checked every door and window in the house. All locked.

The phone rang. She screamed a little at the sound. Angry at herself, she answered with a shout. "That's it, I'm calling the police."

"The secret to your existence is right in front of you. It manifests itself as all those things you know you should do, but are avoiding."

She jammed her pointer finger on the "End Call" button and called 911.

"911, what's your emergency?"

"Oh thank the goddess," Edie breathed. "Some

maniac won't stop calling me. I'm home alone and it's raining and he sounds like a Canadian Kermit the Frog knock off. Please send someone. *Please.*"

"Calm down ma'am, I'm dispatching the police to your location now. Is the cell phone you're calling me with right now the one receiving the threatening calls?"

"Yes." Edie backed her way from the living room to the kitchen, stopping to scoop Baxter into her free arm.

"Okay, ma'am, you need to leave now. Run. We traced the calls, and they're coming from *inside the house.*"

With a flicker, the kitchen light died, and a disembodied voice drifted through the room.

"You carry character with you wherever you go, and it allows you to prevail against adversity."

Pull the Plug

"He did it again," said my son, Angel. "He grimaced."

"You're imagining things," answered Angela, his twin sister. "They've got him on so many pain meds he might as well be gone already."

She was right, and she was wrong. I was so medicated my soul felt detached from my body, but I *had* grimaced. They weren't enough, the drugs. I needed release.

"I wish he was," said Angel.

"Don't talk like that."

"Why not? I put a pillow over the mic they hid in the TV remote." He looked at me. "He's the reason we have to do that in the first place." He looked back to Angela. "Besides, you were thinking it too."

She didn't deny it, and the remains of my heart broke. My sweet Angela ... Memories rushed back to me. Pushing them on the swings at their first birthday party, timing them so one was always going up when the other was coming down. Teaching them cursive in grade school. I might have laughed, if there wasn't a giant tube shoved down my throat. God, how Angel fought me over his school work. I loved that boy so much, the warmth was palpable, even now.

"The damage he caused," continued Angel. "How do we even measure it? You remember when we we were little and got the chicken pox so bad they took us to the hospital? There was *one* hospital, for everyone. Not this ... this ... bullshit." He mimicked an authority figure, and it took a moment to realize it was me. "'Black people this way, white people that way. Because we have to tear down oppressive -'"

"Stop it!" shouted Angela. "Please." She cried openly now, and I never wanted anything more than to throw my arms around her. "Don't you think I know what he's done? You don't think I see conversations stop when I walk into a room? The fear in people's eyes, just because of my last name?"

The silence following her burst of emotion echoed.

"We could end it," Angel said, almost too softly to hear over the various contraptions keeping me alive.

"Angel! How could you even *think* it? To murder your own father?"

"It's *not* murder. He made us his medical guardians. If we judge it merciful, we can tell the doctors to shut all this crap down and let him die. Like you said, he's on so many pills he might as well be dead."

Angela stared at me. She reached out to grasp my hand, but pulled back. "It *would* be merciful, wouldn't it?"

Angel stiffened. "And what mercy has he ever shown anyone?"

I waited for Angela to defend me. Paralyzed by the bodily carnage my sickness had wrought, I screamed the only place I could.

I did it for you! It was all for you. I molded the world so you would have a place in it.

"I think," she said, "he believed he was doing right. By us, by the world."

Yes! Please, if only I could make you understand.

"Doing right?" spat Angel. "We have segregated neighborhoods again. By law! That son of a bitch brought back redlining and told everyone it was to 'fight gentrification.'" He spun on her. "How many lives were snuffed out because he stood behind all those podiums and demanded we defund the police? Entire neighborhoods are war zones now. You couldn't pay people to move into them, but hey - at least they're safe from integration."

Angela laid a hand on his shoulder. "I know. But he'll be gone soon. Maybe its our lot in life to undo what he's done."

"Yeah, just what I wanted. Enforced purpose. It's what I dreamed about, all those nights I read redacted books, or watched mobs junk another statue." Angel fell into a nearby chair, suddenly exhausted. "Do you know they used to have 'roasts' on television?"

"I heard dad talking about them once. They sounded horrible."

"No! They were hilarious!" He leaned forward, reanimated. "One guest of honor sat there while a line of friends and comedians shredded them. Every single minute of them violated the inclusion and decency rules *he* crafted."

Angela gasped. "You've seen them?"

He nodded. "It wasn't easy, but yeah. And I can tell you, comedy used to be funny." The muscles in his jaw bulged as he stared at me, and I thought he might end it there.

Do it.

The shock of Angel's hatred rended my very being, and I silently plead for the liberation of death.

"And art used to have depth," whispered Angela. "Before every writer and director beat us over the head with tired declarations of righteousness."

No ... not you too. My sweet, beautiful child. I cast my eyes upward. *Dear God, why won't you let me die?*

"Remember that professor we had?" asked Angel. He stood over me again, a tear running freely down his cheek as he stared at me. "Political Science? Mr. Haas. Remember the parallels he drew between the Nazi death camps in 'Man's Search for Meaning,' and the Soviet prison camps in 'The Gulag Archipelago?'"

Angela nodded, but said nothing.

"That was his last semester teaching. I never told you. I knew how you felt about him. I ran into him a few years later, working the cash register at Pizza Palace."

"Oh my god." She covered her mouth. "That's why you refused to go there."

"Our universities are a *joke!* People used to come

from every country on the planet to study here. Now the rest of the world treats our graduates like political officers. Spies. And *he* architected all of it."

The two stood quietly, looking down at me. I begged for forgiveness with every atom of my being. I had no idea they felt this way. How many others? Why hadn't I heard any of this when I could have done something about it?

"So what do we do with him?" asked Angela softly.

Angel leaned over me, and I felt a tear race down my cheek as I saw the contempt etched in his sneer.

"We let him rot."

Tuition ... of Death

I was desperate. Driven to subsistence living by the oppressive debt foisted on me by my alma mater, I reached out in all directions, and all ways. But one of those ways, unbeknownst to me, held both the promise of salvation, and the threat of eternal suffering.

It was during my shift at the grocery store that such dubious help arrived in the form of my Fat Studies professor. We conversed while I bagged her groceries, and as she left, I noticed a business card resting where her garbanzo beans once had. Curious, I glanced at it.

Mammon, Merchant Prince of the Demon World

There was more, but I had work to do, so, thrusting the card into my back pocket, I promptly forgot about it.

By rights, that should have been the end of my story, because I washed those jeans without noticing the card. It was only while pulling them from my parents' dryer that I felt a preternatural chill. The card was right where I'd left it, and entirely whole. Whatever dark magic caused the foul emanation also protected it from the spin cycle.

Squinting in the semi-dark hallway, I flipped the light on. The letters seemed to finish shifting as the glare struck them. The language was foreign, strange, *malevolent*. Without understanding a word of it, I knew I should have been scared.

But I wasn't.

I re-pocketed the card and went about my laundry, but a strange tingling permeated my right buttock. Eventually, clothing half folded, I locked myself in my room and stared at the card. Visions assaulted me, and I convulsed. The sinister words of a long-dead language erupted from my mouth. My soul was paralyzed, damned to witness my body's betrayal as it called forth Mammon, ancient demon of wealth and greed.

My legs collapsed beneath me, forcing me to sit in the manner of antediluvian sorcerers.

Criss cross apple sauce.

I yearned to cry out, to scream for mercy, but my tongue and mouth were not my own. My hands grasped pen and paper, drawing the abomination's sigil as I chanted words I did not - could not - understand. Voice undulating, I gripped the pen and stabbed myself through the palm. Not even the deviant power controlling me could stop my sobbing at the pain as I watched my blood drip on to the sigil.

It came to life, that wretched symbol of archaic heresies. It came to life and it writhed before my eyes. My chanting grew louder, and I intuited the approaching crescendo.

A sharp rapping sounded from my door.

"Honey, we're having chicken for dinner, ready in twenty."

"Thanks mom."

Waves of filth vomited forth, soaking my clothes, my body. I blacked out.

I must have awakened soon after, because my mother yet clanked through the kitchen. But I was not alone. Across from me sat a horned devil made of gold.

"Mammon," I whispered.

He bowed his head in acknowledgment. "I have felt your craving from across the eternal void, human." His voice was less heard than felt, and my head throbbed at his utterances.

"My ... cravings?"

"Do not toy with me, mortal. A bargain must be struck."

And so we bargained. Time's enduring march held no sway within those walls as, over the course of days, I bartered my very soul. Finally, when sanity itself threatened to assault me, Mammon stood.

"Alright then, it sounds like we have a deal." He smiled and shook my hand before executing a complex series of gestures. A swirling oval of darkness appeared over my bed, and Mammon stepped toward it.

Shocked by the demon's rapid change in demeanor, I foolishly quipped at his retreating form. "Wow, I hope your demonic sons don't bargain as hard as their father."

Shadows erupted from the beast, his fury palpable. Waves of malice crashed over me, through me as he turned around. A putrid sourness abused my nostrils, and he spoke the final words my earthly senses would hear.

"Did you just assume my gender?"

Algorithms for Algorithms

It was Jane's fourteenth birthday, a time of trepidation for every youth.

Her parents, following protocol, wheeled her into the surgical center. She was weak from fasting, but moreso from the pre-bottled cocktail parents were compelled to feed their kids. It was preparatory, the guides said.

"I know it's scary, dear," said Jane's mother, "but trust me, life is *so* much easier afterward."

"She's right," added her father. "Things don't seem so complicated anymore. Far more manageable. You'll see."

Jane barely registered their assurances, though some part of her mind screamed, cried, and thrashed like an innocent man on death row. *Man?* Innocent *person* on death row. Or was it man? She wasn't sure which was preferred. She'd soon know.

The surgery was as uneventful as one might expect from a procedure perfected years prior, and performed millions of times since. A tiny scar on her left temple, noticeable because of the conspicuous bald patch, was the the only visible sign she'd done anything more than have a pizza party for her birthday. She was home within hours, resting in the care of her loving parents.

The following day, she awoke sore, and disoriented, but otherwise fine. It was a Saturday, and her parents were on hand to pamper her with

French toast and vegan sausages.

"How do you feel, honey?" asked her mom.

Jane moaned. "Ugh, like someone ki ..." She froze. Red text scrolled down her mom's face, suggesting a non-violent replacement for 'kicked in the head,' the phrase she'd been about to use. She must have looked confused, because her parents redoubled their pampering.

"You get used to it," said her dad. "I used to get in all *sorts* of shenanigans." He chuckled at the memory. "Now, every day sails right past, smooth as," he paused a second, "silk."

Jane stared at them, unable to articulate her thoughts. "How ... *why?*" A tear rolled down one cheek.

Matching tears welled in her parents' eyes, and her mother rushed to hug her. "Because it's better this way." She held her at arms' length and spoke with a depth Jane had never witnessed in her. "You don't know yet what life is like without the implant."

"How can you say that?" Jane fought to control her sobbing, and lost. "I lived my entire life without it until yesterday."

"No," her father said quietly, unable to meet her gaze. "You don't understand yet. If you don't have the implant, no top tier university will accept you." He saw Jane about to speak and lifted a finger in warning. "Stop. Please, listen. They'll *tell you* they will, but they won't. They have so many applicants, it's easy to just ... screen you out." His eyes drifted to his shoes, and Jane saw, for the first time, her father fighting for emotional control.

"You?" she asked.

He nodded. "I was valedictorian. As a teenager I held two patents in robotics. I was rejected from nearly every institution." He lifted his head, but still wouldn't look her in the eyes, staring instead at the wall above her head. "And that wasn't the end of it. After six years at the only college that would have me, I could barely cover rent." He shook his fist, suddenly animated. "A Bachelor's in Computer Science, and a ..." he paused, "no, screw the new phrase, a *Master's* in Artificial Intelligence, and no firm I'd heard of would touch me."

Jane's mother reached for his hand, and he clutched it like a lifeline.

"There's more," her mother said. "Those pictures of you and the family I post on social media? No one used to see them. Well, almost no one. Not before I got this." She tapped her temple. "They weren't banned, or removed. They just never seemed to show up for most people."

"So you put a mind control chip in your daughter's head?" Jane shouted through her tears.

"No!" her father said. "That's not how it works. They couldn't get that through the legal system. Any kind of punishment violated so many human rights accords they couldn't manage it. It just *suggests* things. Phrasing mostly, though it will warn you away from various things. Microaggressions, preferring data to lived experience, things like that."

"It already corrected me," said Jane. "I was going

to say I felt like I'd been kicked in the head, and the stupid thing corrected me before I even said it."

"The algorithm's predictive," said her father, putting a hand on her shoulder. "They update the code monthly, so the preferred terminology is usually up to date, though not always." He offered a rueful smile.

Jane grasped her situation with the same agility that continually got her in trouble at school. "If they update the code, the chip is programmable, and reachable."

A subtle smile crept through her father's features. "It is, and it is."

With a final sniffle, Jane looked at her father, who was finally able to make and hold eye contact. "Then it sounds like we have work to do."

The Critic

Charlotte didn't want to hang herself. At least not most of the time.

In fact, the only time Charlotte *did* want to hang herself was when her husband Sam was around.

"You'd look better with shorter hair."

That was the first suggestion. Charlotte remembered it well, because it came on their one-month anniversary. She hadn't thought much about it at the time, but she thought about it now.

Things had spiraled from there.

"We should change the curtains."
(Charlotte liked the curtains)

"Have you thought about upgrading your phone?"
(Charlotte's phone worked fine)

"This place could use a deep cleaning."
(Charlotte didn't know what that meant, but it sounded like a lot of work)

Sam's suggestions grew increasingly personal with time, and Sam himself grew more insistent. Soon Charlotte found herself waiting until she heard Sam slam the front door on the way out each morning before leaving bed.

Charlotte had a friend, Mandy, and Mandy did not like Sam one bit.

"Why don't you stand up to him?" she asked. "It's *your* house too, tell him you don't *feel* like listening to the style of music he thinks you should, or whatever else he's pushing on you that day. Every time you cave, he gets more obnoxious."

Charlotte knew Mandy was right, and she tried to stand up to Sam, but every time he did, Sam collapsed in a blubbering heap and accused Charlotte of abuse. They had neighbors close enough to hear that racket. Charlotte *had* to back down, before someone called the police. But every time, soon after she apologized, Sam would get back to harping on her about this or that.

Not long after, Sam lost his job. He was furious at the blatant bigotry and harassment he'd faced at work, and swore he had an airtight lawsuit. When Charlotte asked him what, exactly, his boss had said or done, Sam exploded again. Oscillating between anger and despair, he accused Charlotte of being 'part of the problem.'

Sam's unemployment stretched from days, to weeks, to months. Charlotte had tried early on to convince him to forget his lawsuit, which was perpetually on the cusp of going somewhere, and apply for new jobs.

"Look here, a sales associate position," she said.
"Garbage pay. That place abuses its employees," Sam said after a glance.

"Programmer. Entry level. Oh Sam, you'd make more than I do!"
"I can't program, Charlotte, I only took one class and got a C."

"Carpenter's apprentice? The pay is minimal, but after a year -"

"I don't know anything about carpentry."

And so it went. Charlotte suggested dozens of occupations before giving up, with Sam informing her he didn't know how to do *any* of them.

Charlotte made enough to cover expenses, but only barely. Worse, Sam's new schedule allowed him to follow Charlotte around the house, bombarding her with his opinions on everything from current events to her inadequacies as a wife. Finally she snapped, locking herself in the bathroom to weep. He continued his assault through the door, until she screamed her intention to hang herself.

Sam's offensive ground to a halt. She could hear him crying through the door, and opened it to find him huddled on the ground.

"If you want to hang yourself, fine!" He sprang up and rummaged through the nearby closet until he produced a long extension cord, which he fashioned into a noose. "Here, leave me then." He flung the noose at her, following it with more criticism.

Her heart and soul spent, Charlotte shuffled to the living room and looped the cord over the load-bearing beam running through the otherwise open ceiling. As Sam helplessly watched, she fetched a chair, standing on it while she lowered the noose around her neck. She stared at Sam, tears blurring his visage, desperate for him to stop her. He called her too cowardly to face him.

She jumped off the chair, upward, that her neck would snap and spare her the slower death by strangulation. But as she felt her weight land and the noose tighten, the knot slid free. With a wicked thump, Charlotte's head bounced off the floor next to the chair. The room swirled as she laid there. Her head lolled in Sam's direction, and reality crashed through the murkiness of her concussion.

That fucking idiot can't even tie a knot.

Judgment Day

"It started like any other day," the judge told his eight year old grandson. "A cantankerous old woman stood beneath me, swearing she'd done nothing wrong. They all said that. Every one. It's why I had the plaque affixed to the wall behind me. The one that said 'Causing offense *is* an offense.'"

"Is that why we're -"

"Don't interrupt, young man, it's poor manners." The child apologized, and the old man continued. "She'd been brought in on charges of hate speech, of course, after giving a lecture on affirmative action."

The boy gasped. "She criticized it?"

"No, no, nothing so dramatic. She was, as we say, *indelicate*. Some of the older professors think they can still get away with presenting both sides of an issue. As if this were still 2010 or something." The judge harrumphed, and shifted about until he was comfortable. "At any rate, her tenure obviously hadn't protected her to the degree she'd anticipated."

"Good," said the boy. "I hope you threw a book at her."

The old man chuckled at him and reached out to pat his head before remembering himself. "Someone did. My path led me elsewhere. Here."

"But why, grandpa? You still haven't said what you did."

"I was a fool. In my haste to reprimand the prisoner, I asked her …" The old man paused, and choked back his emotion. "I asked her if she would make the same arguments about someone's *sexual preference.*"

The boy gasped again. "Grandpa no! You didn't use the SP word!" He shrank from the elderly man.

"To my everlasting shame, I did."

A tinny voice burst from the speaker next to the table, and echoed through the small room. "Prisoner 87-01159. You have re-offended. Your pending transfer is to be executed immediately and your sentence doubled."

The room's only door opened, and two beefy men entered. One unlocked the judge's shackles from a loop on the table, and the other lifted the prisoner via his armpits.

"Remember my sin," the old man shouted over his shoulder, as he lost sight of his grandson. "Remember my sin, and be the steward of justice I failed to be!"

The door swung shut with a heavy thump, and the boy sat alone, sad. The door opened a few minutes later, and a pleasant woman of perhaps seventy sat across from him, in the seat his grandfather had so recently warmed.

She smiled and offered the boy a biscuit.

The Loneliness of Sainthood

Andy was a lonely man.

His father was a baby boomer who had presided over the ruining of the world. When confronted with America's wealth gap, and climate change, he had no astute, or even competent, defense for his inaction. So Andy cut him off.

His mother, sweet as a Honeycrisp apple, still identified as Catholic, with all the baggage inherent. So Andy cut her off.

His sister was a track star in high school, and did not like competing against trans women. So Andy cut her off.

His friends were mostly white, and were adamant he not call them racist, particularly in public. They disagreed with his new definition of racism. So Andy cut them off.

His POC friends denied being oppressed, though they appreciated his concern. He was unable to crack the false consciousness holding them hostage. So Andy cut them off.

His boss refused Andy's attempts to add social justice to each meeting agenda, and did not even *have* a social media account with which he might demonstrate his opposition to white supremacy, or the patriarchy. So Andy cut him off.

That is how Andy found himself drinking alone in a pub one day, listening to two old men bicker. Taxes, religion, current events ... The men roared and banged the table as they drank. Neither were terribly enlightened, but insisted on opining nonetheless, and since Andy couldn't cut them off, he resigned himself to their ignorance.

After forty five minutes, and several mugs of beer, one man stood and announced he had to get home.

"Give Janey my love, you rough old bastard," said the other. "The grandkids too."

"Alright, you son of a bitch. Same time tomorrow?"

The man at the table nodded, and the other donned his coat and left. The man at the table caught Andy watching him, and raised his mug in greeting. Andy, remembering some of the things the old man had said, quickly turned and faced the bartender. He nursed his beer until he heard the door shut behind him. Sneaking a look, he saw the old man had gone, and he was the only customer left.

Andy returned to his beer, a lonely man.

The Fugitive

Iliam slid down the jagged brick exterior of an abandoned factory outside Boston, panting. The overgrown brush and old dumpster provided cover. For now.

He'd lost track of how long he'd been running, but the sun was high when he started, and now it was the moon that threatened to undo him. He heard voices in the distance. A chain link fence shook.

Damn them, why can't they let me live!

Dipping into reserves he never knew existed, he shoved himself to his feet and lurched on. A door ahead promised salvation. Locked. Iliam eyed the window panes next to it. The men were closer now. He could make out words. See the beams of their flashlights. He had to decide now.

A brave man only dies once, but a coward dies every day.

With that, he elbowed the pane closest to the door, wincing at the noise. Men shouted, and he reached through the hole to unlock the deadbolt. He flung the door open as the first pursuer rounded the corner, disappearing inside.

"Here!" shouted the man. "He's here!"

Iliam searched his surroundings in a panic. An old plank of wood lay nearby, just larger than a baseball bat. It would have to do. He locked the door, steadied himself a few feet back from it, and waited, club in hand. It wasn't long. The door shuddered as the first few men kicked at it, before noticing the window. An arm groped its way through the breach. Iliam struck.

"Ahhh! My arm! I think he broke my arm!" screamed a voice.

"Iliam, come on out of there," yelled another.

"Let me go," he shouted back. "I don't want to hurt anybody, but I will."

"Would you stop being so dramatic?" the second voice answered. "You signed the contract. No one tricked you. Now payment's due."

Terror gripped Iliam. His makeshift bat clattered to the ground. "No! Never!" He whirled and sprinted away.

A face appeared in the broken pane. "He's headed toward the front. Candesse'll get him."

The men circled back to the front of the building, where Candesse sat upon the squirming Iliam's stomach, knees pinned to either side of him. "Can you stop it? Good lord, it's not that bad. I've done it." She pointed to the group of men. "Cole's done it, John's done it, plenty of us have done it. Heck, I did it in high school!"

"Okay," wheezed Iliam. "You win. God help me, you win." He started to sob.

"Are you kidd... you know what? I don't care. If I let you up, you promise not to run?"

Iliam nodded.

"I'm trusting you ..." Candesse stood and offered Iliam her hand.

He studied the hand, then accepted her help. Once standing, he accidentally locked eyes with her.

"No, no, no you don't!" shouted Candesse as Iliam bolted.

This time Cole was waiting, and wrapped his arms around Iliam's waist. "Hurry! I can't hold him!"

"I think he rubbed baby oil on his arms," said Candesse, arriving with the rest of the men. With the additional support, they bound Iliam while one called for a car. A limousine soon arrived, and Iliam was ushered into it. Immobilized. Helpless. The limousine sped across the city, heedless of traffic lights or speed limits.

Candesse produced a cell phone and dialed. "Yeah, we got him." She paused. "I know, right?" She looked at Iliam and laughed. "Oh man, remind me to tell you about the baby oil." She laughed some more and hung up before turning to Iliam. "You, my friend, are quite the runner."

Iliam squeezed his eyes, willing it all to be one giant nightmare. But it wasn't. Rough hands jostled him from the limo, dragging him through cavernous, deserted hallways toward an ever-growing noise. Panic exploded, and Iliam fought once more, exhausted as he was. It was useless. As he sagged, barely able to stand, someone cut his bonds and shoved him through a massive pair of curtains.

The stage light blinded him, and he lifted a

shielding hand. Polite applause assailed him as an unseen speaker intoned his doom.

"Here he is, ladies and gentlemen. Please welcome, in his first public debate ever, Doctor Iliam, who'll be defending his book on Critical Race Theory tonight."

Zing!

The audience was split, and the man felt it. He smiled. He was about to change that.

"Thank you for telling me how I should feel, I bet that makes you real popular with your wife." He grinned and waited for the applause.

zing

The grin slid from his face at the whispered word, even as the audience laughed and cheered. His opponent sputtered, clearly having a rebuttal he wished to deploy, but having to wait for quiet gave him a helpless, foolish appearance.

Eventually the host of the show calmed the audience enough for the debate to move along. The man's opponent spoke fast, and was well informed. The man was not used to that, and the heat emanating from beneath his collar distracted him.

"If you look at the statistics resulting from the policies you're proposing," said his opponent, "they have the opposite affect to the one you say you want to achieve. If we're measuring racism by outcome and not intention, your policy proposal is racist."

The man wondered how his opponent spoke so quickly, but shook the thought away. The distraction cost him a precious second, and knowing he was a step behind flustered him further. Desperate, he pulled another ace from his sleeve.

"So a white man is going to lecture me about

racism now?"

Zing

It was louder. Clear. The audience howled its joy, and the frustration on his opponent's face ought to have given him a crisp satisfaction. It always did. But that whisper ...

His opponent was undeterred. "It's not a lecture to remind you of your own position on what constitutes racism. Nor is the ability to read statistics incumbent upon skin color."

They battled across several points, and the man regained his confidence. He would focus on issues moving forward, and discreetly inquire about the whisper afterward.

"So," his opponent continued, "if I'm in favor of the rioters from my side being prosecuted and going to jail, and I'm in favor of the rioters from *your* side being prosecuted and going to jail, what are we arguing about? Are you not in favor of applying basic equality under the law to people because you like their opinions?"

The man was ready this time, and he immediately chuckled. "Is this what you do on your show? Because it sucks."[3]

ZING! ZING!

He blinked and shook his head. His opponent noticed, but moved on, reacting with a cheap shot of his own, then cocking his head, a puzzled look on his

---

[3] Web Search: "Shapiro Nance Maher because it sucks"

face. The man tried to enjoy his opponent's descent into the mud, but the whispering didn't stop. It was many voices now, some the faintest of murmurs, others frighteningly aggressive.

"Are you okay?" asked the host.

The man felt dizzy, and clutched the podium for support. "You mad, bro?" he managed to gasp.

ZingzIngZINGzinGZiNGzingZinGZINg

The man dropped to a knee, unable to hear anything beyond *zing*, let alone the desired accolades. His vision narrowed.

The host and his opponent were suddenly beside him, hoisting him to his feet and holding him upright. He leaned on the podium in desperation, and the microphone jabbed him in the cheek.

"I'm sorry," he mumbled.

The men propping him up shared a look of concern.

"It's fine," said the host, "you don't have to apologize for a health problem."

"No," said the man, stronger this time. "I'm sorry." The voices dropped some decibels, but persisted. The man grabbed the microphone and put it to his lips. "My opponent has some valid points. I'd like to see where our views overlap, and work on solutions that improve people's lives. We'll disagree in many areas, but we'll try."

The whispering stopped.

Fog of the Damned

No one noticed it, not at first. Silent and slow, it hugged the ground. Its effects were subtle, and its victims fully encompassed before they perceived the danger.

The fog came for the children first.

I knew something was amiss at the lack of laughter. Hordes of teenagers milled about in a near-fugue state, with nary a demeaning wisecrack. It was difficult to interpret, as the *truly* demeaning comments spilled forth unabated. But the ones between friends were tempered. Neutered.

Not understanding the beast, I had no method with which to combat it, and thus I fled. I fled to college, only to find its sinewy tentacles had already reached those ill-fated young adults. Every conversation, every lecture, every casual exchange, it was there, a suffocating pressure. Nearly imperceptible to the eye, my peers felt it. In hushed tones and small, trusted circles, they spoke of it.

It was during one such lecture I began to grasp the beast's nature. The professor, a well-respected man of perhaps sixty, slipped in his prose. A chill settled upon us all, and yet, seated near the front as I was, I watched a bead of sweat form at his hairline. It slipped downward, past his temple, his cheek, and hung upon his jaw. The fellow moved not a muscle to relieve his cheek of the unbecoming moisture.

My soul yearned to burst from its corporeal home, to save this good man, though from what I did not know. And so I looked. For the first time, I truly looked, and saw the acolytes of the beast among us.

No robes, no markings, no ceremonial instrumentation announced their foul loyalties. Nonetheless it was clear who they were. We all felt it, our very beings recoiling from the mystical and terrifying combination of fire and ice emanating from them.

The fog. Whatever beast had swallowed the children's laughter had long since subdued this campus.

After the professor was hounded from his position, I fled again. Thinking to expose the sinister plot, I found a junior position at a prestigious newspaper. I excelled at the menial tasks before me, and pursued the monster after hours. With the memory of my professor's fall etched into my soul, I quietly studied my colleagues as I worked. To my horror, I realized I was perhaps the only person under forty not under the beast's sway.

I began mouthing the ritual phrases used by the demon's anointed, and thus passed among them unnoticed. I watched, helpless, as they converted or dispatched any who thwarted the monster's capricious desires. Those who crossed it by happenstance were afforded no special quarter. Eager to appease the beast, I augmented my chants with magical pronouns in official correspondence.

As for my quest to uncover the beast's origins and, crucially, its weaknesses, I made no headway. For it was clever, and many-headed. It had spent decades quietly laying the foundation for its supremacy. While society worked to improve itself incrementally, it seeded the fields of those institutions necessary for the next generations to continue.

I despaired in my quest to unmake the fiend. I was too late, too insignificant. Where the fog laid claim, laughter, goodwill, and humanity were banished. On credible pretenses I departed with bold intentions.

If the beast could not be ejected from our institutions, we would found replacements. In secret at first, quietly gathering those brave few capable of resisting one evil without turning to another. We would marshal our resources, build our strength. In time, we would challenge the beast from a position of power.

We would yet again hear the laughter of children.

The Test

Alan tried to log in. He really did.

His username was right. His password was the same as it was everywhere else. But Alan couldn't log in.

It was that damned captcha. *It's just a check box, how could they screw this up?* His mouse pointer hovered over it, but every time he clicked, the pointer jumped, and he missed.

Frustrated, Alan called the help number.

"Customer support, this is Tina. How can I help you?" answered a friendly voice.

"Hi Tina, before we start, do you identify as a woman? I want to make sure I don't misgender you."

"I do, sir. What seems to be the problem?"

"My first problem is the cisnormative assumption that you know my preferred pronouns," he said.

"Ahh, okay. Trouble logging in?"

Alan was confused about how Tina knew that, but grunted a yes, describing the faulty captcha and affirming his pronouns.

"No problem, sir. Let me pull up the troubleshooting steps." There was a slight pause. "Sir, is racism about race, or about power?"

Caught unaware, it took Alan a moment to answer. "Power of course. Prejudice without power isn't racism. That's why only white people can be racist."

"I see. And is gender real?"

"No, it's a social construct."

"Good, good." Alan heard her typing. "One final question, sir. What differences, if any, are there between men and women?"

"Why, there isn't a lick of difference!" he cried. "How is any of this useful? I'm trying to log into your web site, not teach you basic morality. Help me get past your broken captcha or let me talk to your supervisor."

"Sir, can you please read the broken captcha to me?"

"I certainly can. It says, 'I am not a robot.'"

"Sir, the captcha isn't broken."

High Beams

The girl in the Cadillac Escalade went to the most expensive private school in New York state. She drove there one Friday night to protest the systemic racism of the school's basketball program. As she drove away from the parking lot, she saw a pick up truck leave behind her.

Blech, how is that thing even running?

She noticed it following her. When she sped up, it sped up, though it seemed to top out around sixty miles per hour. When she passed a car, it passed a car. Thinking it amusing, she slowed down enough for it to keep up. Then it flashed its high beams at her. She tapped a button on her phone.

"Call daddy."

The phone dialed her father.

"Yes honey?" came his voice.

"Daddy a truck is following me. It … it just did it again! It's flashing its high beams at me."

"Calm down, honey. How far away are you?"

"Five minutes. Should I speed up? I don't think it can keep up. Oh daddy, I saw it parked. It had an American flag sticker on it."

Her father paused. "This is more serious than I thought. Don't speed or drive erratically. I'll alert the security detail. Pull into the car park as usual."

The girl followed her father's instructions, though it was difficult not to panic. Every minute or so, the truck turned its high beams on, only to turn them off after a few seconds.

Finally, the girl turned on to her driveway.

Only a quarter mile until safety.

She couldn't resist accelerating the last acre, and barely skidded to a halt before running from the car. The truck followed suit, and a rather plain young man leapt from the it, shouting and pointing at the Escalade.

"He's in the back seat! There's a man in - Ahhh!" He fell as a security guard tasered him.

Just then, a movement caught the girl's eye. "Daddy look." She pointed to her Cadillac. Security converged, pulling a frightful maniac from the SUV.

"He got into - Ahhhh! Stop tasing me! He slipped into the back seat in the parking lot. *Without a mask.* I couldn't stop him in time, so I followed you. Every time he was about to talk to you, I turned my high beams on and he dropped back down, afraid someone would see him."

The Big Sleep

The year was 2032, and Angela was confused.

When her favorite basketball team ran on to the court, not one signaled their political beliefs. Not. One. Nevertheless, she continued watching.

It was a magnificent game, a nail-biter, won by a free throw. She waited for the post-game interview. The hero of the day thanked his teammates. He praised his coach, and complimented the opposing team. No one else seemed perturbed.

And Angela was confused.

Several days later, she watched her first football game in nearly a decade. *This will be different.* Except it wasn't. The teams both jogged on to the field with nary a banner or symbol to be found. The National Anthem played, and she grew excited. But no one knelt. Some sat, some stood, some held their hands over their hearts. The commentators discussed the game, the players, and various strategies.

And Angela was confused.

The pattern repeated itself in every sport Angela cared to watch.

Boxing: no slogans or lectures.
Hockey: only burly men on skates, playing the game the best they could.
NASCAR: just driving, with several unfortunate mishaps.

And Angela was confused.

Where were the slogans on jerseys? Where were the gestures, the verbal cues, the signs in the crowd? Why was every post-game interview about the sport? Who was forcing commentators to compliment the athletes on their amazing physical prowess, their tactical acumen, and their dedication to their craft, while constraining their ability to question the athletes motives, or political allegiances?

The Olympics came that year, and Angela was confused. So confused that she walked back into the hospital room she'd slumbered in for nine years.

"Hi Frank," she said to her comatose neighbor, as she laid down in the oddly familiar bed. "I'm back."

The Job Interview

"Tell me about your experience."

Jenny was flustered. She hadn't expected to be pressed so rudely, and by a friend of her father's, no less.

"Kind sir," she said, "surely you see right there on the page. I went to a top university."

"Yes, madam," he answered. "It is a fine university indeed."

Jenny smiled, glad that was settled.

"But I'm afraid I must insist," the man continued, "that you describe your relevant experience."

Taken aback, Jenny reminded herself that she mustn't expect Ivy League manners from one such as he. "Sir, I thought I made myself clear. As is evident, I have a Master's degree."

The man adjusted his bifocals and studied her resume anew. "Ahh yes, I see. Now, about that experience?"

She felt her patience trickling away. "I believe I've answered your question, and would ask that you please move on."

With a gentle nod, the man traced a finger down the page, frowning as he reached the bottom. "Might I ask, what relevant skills would you bring to the firm?"

"I am skilled in many ways, sir. Can you please be more specific?"

"Can you perchance fix my computer?"

"No, sir, I cannot."

"No bother, that. Have you created an advertising or marketing campaign?"

"I wasn't aware there was a difference."

"Certainly," the man mumbled, tapping his chin, "'tis confusing to me as well." He looked up suddenly with a hint of cheer. "I don't suppose you know Javascript, do you?"

"No."

"Have you a mind for legalese?"

Jenny shook her head.

The man placed her resume neatly on the desk and removed his glasses. He fixed her with a stern eye. "Madam, you must help me help you. Please describe something impressive you have done, that I might find a role for you."

With no small amount of pride, Jenny lifted her chin. "I led multiple rallies, both on and off campus, sir. As the head of our university's Junior ACLU club, I ensured the safety of the student body by intervening directly when undesirables threatened to lecture there. I dare say I was fundamental in shaping many students' views on tolerance, whilst protecting them from speech that might spread, incite, promote, or justify hatred, violence, and discrimination against a person or group of persons[4]."

The man rocked back in his chair, suitably impressed. "Well then, I dare say you've the makings of a fine Human Resources specialist. We don't have any openings at the moment, but I can pull some strings for a lass of such upstanding moral quality." He winked at her. "Founder's prerogative."

They stood, and the man walked her to the lobby.

"I look forward to seeing you in these proud halls, amidst the hand-chosen men and women that have made this company feel more like a second family." He leaned toward her and dropped his voice. "If you're not careful, you may end up married. We've celebrated two weddings between colleagues in as many years."

Jenny momentarily froze as her brain processed the heteronormative assault on her personhood. Recovering quickly, she smiled and thanked the man with a handshake. She would take this job, she thought. She would take this job, she would disrupt the patriarchy from within, and she would start with *him*.

---

[4] Hate speech definition swiped from: https://newdiscourses.com/tftw-hate-speech/

Erased

I looked strange. Shaving this morning, I looked strange. Like I was the same, but something was slightly different. I stood in front of the mirror, scraping a razor across my jaw, distracted by … what?

Driving to work was no better. I nearly rear ended the woman in front of me because I was fixated on my hand. It seemed to take the color of the steering wheel, but only when I wasn't looking directly at it.

I clocked in late, having sat examining myself in the rear view mirror for some unknown number of minutes before a coworker tapped on my window. Strapping my apron on, I planted a dead-eyed grin on my face to greet my first customer.

"Large coffee please."

I rang him up wrong, startled to discover my fingers had become translucent.

"I'll finish your order, sir." My manager stepped between me and the cash register. He finished, and turned to eye me. "What's wrong with you? You've been acting weird since the staff meeting last night."

I tried to answer. My mouth moved, but no sound emerged. Terrified, I ran to the break room. *Tears.* I was crying, why did I not feel tears on my cheek?

My manager followed, eleventh-hour concern scrawled across his face.

He did this to me.

"Is this about that diversity training you wanted me to assign everyone?"

It was too late. I understood, but it was too late. My final sensation was my shirt, devoid of corporeal impediment, drifting to the floor.

The Hotel Room

Well past midnight, a man entered his hotel room alone He noticed it had a coffee machine.

Odd, that should be a Cappuccino maker.

Suspicious, he checked the room number on the door. It was the right room. He scratched at the blue flag underneath the number. Nothing fishy there.

Unwilling to make a fuss, the man kicked his shoes off and flopped on the bed.

A little TV to rest the brain.

He pointed the remote, hit power, and eased into the feathery abundance of pillows. Such a long flight. The fussy brat behind him made sure he didn't sleep. He felt himself drifting ... drifting ...

"And that's why the Democrats refuse to talk about the steep decline in Covid deaths."

Terror pierced the man's fatigued mind, jolting him awake.

Fox News. The default channel should be CNN. Unless ...

He leapt from the bed, turning a slow circle in the middle of the room. His eyes settled on the bedside table.

No ... Please Gaia, no.

His hand crept toward the drawer, stopping several times before he mustered the courage to slide it open. A Bible!

The walls closed in. Or did they? He felt himself losing consciousness, and fought his way to the bathroom. Staggering to the sink, he splashed cold water repeatedly into his face. His pulse slowed.

It's just a misunderstanding. Nothing more. Just a misunderstanding. Someone made a mistake.

He reached for the nearest towel and used it to dry his face. As he pulled it away, he realized his danger. There, in a frame next to the mirror … an AMERICAN FLAG.

Unable to breath, he sprinted from the room, not stopping until he reached the front desk. A lone clerk greeted him as he clung to the check-in counter, panting.

"Good evening, anything I can do for you, sir? Oh, I'm sorry." The clerk leaned across the counter and smiled. *Were those fangs?* "I didn't catch your preferred pronouns."

Moving Day

"I'm glad you decided to help," said Charles.

"No worries," Phil answered. "Moving sucks." He yanked his t-shirt from the front pocket of his shorts and mopped it across his forehead. "Let's get this done."

Charles frowned and turned away, but said nothing as they hoisted his couch. They twisted and fought with it until it fit through the door, walking it halfway down the stairs before gently placing it down for a breather.

"This is a good start," said Charles, sitting on the stairs above Phil.

"What do you mean?"

"At evening things out."

Phil looked up at Charles, one hand shielding his eyes from the sun. "What are you talking about?"

"I know you feel like you owe me this, and honestly, you kinda do. I'm just saying, it's a good start."

"I'll ask again. What in the bloody blue hell are you talking about?" asked Phil. "I don't owe you squat."

"Sure." Charles smiled into the distance. "Let's get this thing loaded, eh?"

Phil's mood had curdled in the last thirty seconds,

but he'd agreed to help his friend, so help he did. They wrestled the couch into the large, rented truck, grabbed the dolly, and went back for the fridge.

"This ought," Charles grunted as they eased it down each stair, "to work ... off ... some guilt."

"Guilt ... for what?" Phil grunted back.

They reached the bottom of the stairs and leaned on the fridge until they stopped panting.

"For all the times you didn't help," said Charles.

"Are you kidding me with this crap? I'm helping you move on a sunny Saturday afternoon and you're bitching about all the times I *should* have helped you before?"

"Don't be so sensitive, man. I'm just saying ..." He splayed his hands out toward Phil. "You had a lot of benefits growing up that I didn't."

Phil leaned against the dolly and stared at Charles. "Yeah, I had it easier than you. So what? I'm here. Now. Helping you."

"Because of the guilt."

"What guilt? I didn't do anything to feel guilty about. I'm here because I like you and you needed help. And I'm not so sure about the 'liking' bit right now."

"And I'm what? Supposed to thank you for finally noticing I needed help?"

"All things considered, yeah. A simple 'thank you,'

seems reasonable. I never did you wrong, and here I am, trying to help." He paused as a thought struck him. "Have you always had this much contempt for me?"

"Wow, fragile much?"

"Frag ... You know what? I don't owe you shit, and I'm done being insulted." He jerked his shirt from his pocket and pulled it over his head. "Let me know when you grow up."

"Oh, that's right," said Charles. "Run away as soon someone makes you uncomfortable."

"I'm not uncomfortable, I'm pissed off. At you. And I was just going to leave. But since you couldn't keep your mouth shut, that's my dolly, and I'm taking it with me." He unstrapped the fridge, freed his dolly, and pushed it down the driveway. "Have fun doing it by yourself."

When the Music's Over

He wasn't always like this. He used to be funny. In fact, he'd been making people laugh his entire life, with a wit so cutting he'd nearly been expelled multiple times. And probably would have been if a few choice comments hadn't sailed over his teachers' heads.

It was only over the last few years he began to dread the day upon waking. A precious second or two after reemerging into consciousness was his only respite.

He was a fraud.

His wife, the only person who knew he was struggling, assured him it was all in his mind, but he knew. The same wit that almost got him expelled as a teenager had also propelled him upward in the world of comedy, upward to the pinnacle of success. And that wit was, by necessity, propelled by an intellect, coupled with an ability to read people, that denied him solace in polite lies.

Which was why his eyes rested on the pistol beside him.

Foreign tears moistened those eyes now, blurring the image as he pondered how long he'd been miserable. It hadn't started with his new show, not immediately, but the two were bound.

He'd paid his dues on the stand-up comedy circuit, but unlike most comedians, he'd quickly found a niche on cable TV. He conceived and delivered punchlines quicker than most people could process what flew from his mouth, and for that the people loved him. But more crucial, he now grasped, was that he *believed* in what he did. That belief made his seemingly inevitable late night talk show an obvious win.

It was a trap.

Despite the supercomputer between his ears - *with a math co-processor*, he chuckled through the pain - he couldn't pin his descent to any single, pivotal moment. Every step felt natural, even in hindsight. Like a hiker following a game trail, only to find themselves alone and shivering when they finally stopped to rest.

He heard his wife's voice in his mind. "If you hiked there, you can turn around and hike back."

His gaze drifted to the opening monologue, stacked neatly beside the pistol. Maybe he could. Maybe he *could* hike back. Maybe he *could* deliver a monologue that just ... entertained people, instead of haranguing them. Lecturing them. Delivering a political sermon barely disguised as humor. Grabbing the notes, he flung them across the room. He didn't need to read them, they were entirely predictable. He'd read the top five headlines of the day, and he knew what his audience expected. Nay, *demanded*. With one mental lurch he combined the headlines and expectations, and his brain vomited an opening monologue so predictable and self righteous he had to tamp down the urge to use the pistol right then.

What happened to me?

His breath quickened, became shallow.

Panic attack.

He ran through the Cognitive Behavioral Therapy steps his therapist taught him. His family loved him. He was healthy. Millions of people adored him. His brain rejected the last one, pointing out that they only loved him because of that fucking monologue strewn across the room. He never could lie to himself. Money! He had more than he needed. No matter what happened, he and his family would survive, intact. Mostly.

Family. Health. Money. His breathing slowed, though the tears dripping from his cheeks to wet the slacks of his tailored suit neglected to stop.

Looking from the script to the gun, he knew the moment had come. There was no picking up one without picking up the other. He might stave off any lethal impulses for a night. A week. He doubted he'd make it a month. But he knew, the script and the gun were a package deal.

Terrified and ashamed, he chose.

The Whimsical

Call Me Ishmael ...

"A lot of people have asked me about them, so I figured I'd explain my pronouns," said Sam. He paced back and forth, a little nervous. He'd never enunciated his full thinking to anyone else, though she'd practiced many times alone.

"I like my pronouns being used interchangeably. My *default* is 'they/them,' but like, sometimes I have more femme days. Then I go by 'she/her.' Other days I feel more masculine, so I use 'he/him.'"

They looked around for questions and, finding none, galloped onward.

"Some days I float between pronouns, so I'm getting pins to wear." Sam held up a pin that said 'they,' then flipped it upside down so it read 'she.' "Obviously this one doesn't cover all my pronouns so I'm getting new ones made." He paused to smile reassuringly. "I'm pretty flexible, just don't use 'it' or any neopronouns, okay?"

Hasini, his audience of one, stared at him from the other side of the counter with a loaf of bread in each gloved hand. "I'm sorry," she said, her accent thicker with emotion as tears threatened to spill from her eyes. "I don't understand anything you said. Please, just tell me what kind of bread you want for your sandwich."

New Cat, Same Cradle

The punchline arrived just the other day
It landed with a smack in the usual way
But it insulted the church, and offended me
So I explained the reason that it wasn't funny
And he self censored 'fore I knew it, as he grew
He'd say "I'm gonna be like you dad
You know I'm gonna be like you"

And the cat's in the cradle and the activist
Little boy blue and the threatening fist
When you gonna laugh dad?
I don't know when, but I'll be a fun guy then
You know we'll have a good time then

My son turned ten just the other day
He said, "Thanks for the sermon, Dad, come on let's play
Can you teach me a joke", I said "Not today
I got some yelling to do", he said, "That's okay"
And he walked away but his smile never dimmed
And said, "I'm gonna be like him, yeah
You know I'm gonna be like him"

And the cat's in the cradle and the activist
Little boy blue and the threatening fist
When you gonna laugh dad?
I don't know when, but I'll be a fun guy then
You know we'll have a good time then

Well, he came home from college just the other day
So much like a man I just had to say
"Son, I'm proud of you, can we share a chuckle?"
He shook his head and he cracked a knuckle
"What I'd really like, Dad, it to go to a protest

Don't wait up, there's gonna be some unrest."

And the cat's in the cradle and the activist
Little boy blue and the threatening fist
When you gonna laugh son?
I don't know when, but I'll be a fun guy then dad
You know we'll have a good time then

I've long since retired, my son's moved away
I called him up just the other day
I said, "I'd like to see a stand up comedy bit"
He said, "I'd love to dad, but we cancelled it
The guy insulted some friends and he got his due
But it's sure nice talking to you, Dad
It's been sure nice talking to you"

And as I hung up the phone it occurred to me
He'd grown up just like me
My boy was just like me

And the cat's in the cradle and the activist
Little boy blue and the threatening fist
When you gonna laugh son?
I don't know when, but I'll be a fun guy then dad
You know we'll have a good time then

Groundhog's Dinner

"Racism is prejudice plus power," said Kendra.

Her parents looked at each other.

"Yes, we heard you the first time," said her mother, Ellie. "We just disagree."

Her father, Dave, wiped one corner of his mouth and placed his cloth napkin back on the table. "The idea that someone can openly hate another person for their skin color and it *isn't* racism doesn't sit right with me."

"It's about power. Only white people have the power to codify their prejudices into law, and the various bureaucracies. That's why racism is systemic."

"We've been over this Kendra, my boss is Indian. His boss is an Asian woman. This is an 'at-will' employment state - either one of them could fire me tomorrow. These theories they're teaching you are ridiculous."

"Just because you can point to exceptions doesn't mean the system as a whole looks like what you're seeing. Black people have to be exceptional just to be acknowledged."

"No, they don't. My best friend at work is black, and he's not exceptional. I mean, he's *pretty good*, but he's doing just fine. It sounds like your professor is looking at his parents' America."

Kendra sighed and neatly placed her fork beside her knife. "You're cherry picking again. Professor Rybin said you'd do that."

"Honey," said Ellie, "Professor Rybin also said that 'lived experiences' were just as valuable as statistics. Your father is sharing his lived experience with you right now." She looked at her husband. "Isn't a lived experience just an experience? This whole thing seems designed to confuse."

"The lived experiences of marginalized peoples must be prioritized," said Kendra.

Ellie shot a concerned glance at her husband. "That's the third time you've said that. Are you feeling okay?"

"I'm fine, mom. All this emotional labor is really tiring, that's all."

"Emotional labor?" she asked.

"Wait a minute." Dave put his knife and fork down and leaned over his dinner. "My 'lived experiences' don't count because of the color of my skin? What's my role in all this? Just sit there and shut up no matter what anyone says or does? Who's being racist *now?*"

"Racism is prejudice plus power."

A Simple Matter of Measurement

"That's not a real answer," said the pollster.

Joel folded his arms across his chest. "It's the answer I've got."

"Are you refusing to answer?"

"No, I answered you. You just didn't like the answer."

The pollster sighed and reclined in the office chair. "Look, we can do this all day, but *your* union hired me to gather this data, so when I tell them you wouldn't cooperate …"

"I *did* cooperate. And if you want to do this all day, I'll need to let Sheila out front know we'll need a substitute teacher." Joel stood up and took a step toward the door, maintaining eye contact with the man across the table. "We doing this?"

They locked eyes and battled for several seconds, before the pollster turned away.

"Fine, whatever. I'll ask my supervisor how to score you."

"Well then, you have yourself a fine day." Joel left.

The pollster cursed under his breath as he dialed his boss. He'd been getting more of these types lately.

"Hi Justin, it's me, I got another one." He paused. "No, nothing actionable. He was pretty polite, actually. Well, minus his answer." Another pause. "Yeah, just one answer for every question, and I'm not sure we can quantify his white privilege based on it." Another pause. "All he'd say was, 'stick it up your ass.'"

The Unbreakable Bodice

Alice was running out of patience.

She could see William liked her, everyone could. Their small office of some thirty employees had a monthly pool, wherein everyone bet which day Alice and William would finally get together.

The dance had endured for more than a year, and each month, fewer coworkers bothered to gamble on the romantic fruition.

"Why don't you let me set you up with my cousin," asked Bethany one crisp December morning. She paused for another drag of her cigarette. "He's not much, to be honest, but at least he'll make a move. What do you even see in William?"

"He's sweet," said Alice, waving the latest stinky cloud away. She didn't smoke, but liked to get away from her desk once an hour nonetheless. "He's probably the only guy in the office who didn't get metoo'd."

"Okay, you got me there." Bethany stubbed her butt out in the ashtray and they headed inside. "Hey, let's get him drunk at the Christmas party."

"Um, remember the whole 'metoo' thing I just mentioned?"

"Right, right. Well we have to do *something*."

Alice, more cognizant than most of what needed to happen, stayed quiet.

In the build up to the holiday party, Alice made a point to happen across William's area more often. She pulled several of her blouses from storage, the ones she'd worn in her early twenties, that invited a few too many lingering eyeballs. She even wore heels. William was the perfect gentleman. So adept at behaving was he that it fell to Bethany, watching from afar, to tell Alice he'd noticed her in the first place. After that, she felt silly, like a con artist passing signs back and forth to her partner in one of those poker movies.

The night of the party arrived. The office manager, well aware that his employees planned to imbibe that night, had arranged a ride service to take each home as requested. Not much work got done that day, and by three o'clock, most the office was bouncing from cubicle to cubicle, chatting about everything from holiday plans to the latest video game they were playing. Wherever William was, Alice made sure she was nearby.

Hovering. The word is hovering.

Soon the first bottle appeared, and the casual neglect of job duties matured to an enthusiastic party. Alice, despite admonishing Bethany for suggesting the dirty ploy, contributed a bottle of Jagermeister. She'd heard many a tale begin with the word 'Jagermeister.'

Bethany smirked at her behind William's back, and goaded the sedate man into toasting the Christmas spirit. Within minutes, she'd pestered and teased him into another two shots. Alice, having quaffed a few of her own, recognized the moment. Not just to act, but to intervene, and save William from alcohol poisoning.

She mustered her liquid courage and tapped him on the shoulder. "Can I talk to you?" William acquiesced, and she led him to a quiet corner of the office, ignoring the knowing smiles and poorly concealed stares. Being unaccustomed to strong drink, her head swam as she turned to face him. "Why haven't you asked me out?" Her cheeks flushed at the words. She never spoke like this! But there it was, out there. She beat down the urge to dilute her words, or take them back.

"I ... I ... I didn't want to impose," blurted William, his face redder than hers.

"Impose?"

"That's not the right word. I'm sorry. God, I'm so bad at this."

Alice intervened again. "Do you mean harass? Like you didn't want to harass me?"

He gave a relieved nod.

"William, that's very sweet, but you could have just asked me for a cup of coffee."

"Oh no." He shook his head, eyes glued to the nearby desk, as if the dirty keyboard and random junk suddenly fascinated him. "I couldn't risk making you uncomfortable. You have to come into work every day! What if you -"

"William." He stopped babbling and looked her in the eyes as she continued. "It's just coffee. And it's not harassment if you accept 'no' and don't ask again." Still amazed at her own prowess, she decided to go for broke. "Watch me do it." She took one large step backwards. "Hi William, I was thinking of getting some coffee, would you like to come with?" She bowed.

"I, um," he saw her face falter. "Yes! I do. It's just that I'm a manager."

"Not mine."

"I know, but I'm friends with Frank," he said, referring to Alice's manager. "You might feel pressured to -"

"I don't."

"Yes, but how do I *know* that?"

Alice fought the urge to sigh. Maybe it was the alcohol, but William's cute and coy routine was beginning to grate on her. "You know because I'm *telling* you." Skepticism wafted from him. "William, I'm not made of glass. Honestly? This is getting a little insulting."

"Oh geez, I didn't mean to insult you. I was afraid this would happen."

Alice ground her teeth. "Focus, William. Coffee. Do you want it?" At this point she wasn't sure *she* did, but it seemed silly to come this far, only to pull the ripcord because of two annoying minutes.

"I do. Let me go talk to Wanda first though. I just want to clear it with Human Resources to make sure -"

She'd had enough. Spinning on her heels, Alice stomped back to the party, leaving William to stammer on about improprieties.

Bethany intercepted her before she reached the main group. "You look mad. What happened? Did he get handsy?"

Alice shook her head and tried to form her thoughts into something coherent. Frustration at William, and her own inability to articulate the problem, bubbled out in the form of unvarnished truth.

"What a pussy."

Serenity Now

"I'm thrilled at the confidence you have in me," said the young director, "but I must admit, I'm a little confused. Why would we reboot Serenity? The movie is barely fifteen years old."

A man in his forties raised his pointer finger. "I can take this one." He stood and paced toward the director, stopping halfway around the massive, oak table. "We feel the movie isn't in line with today's values."

"It was released in 2005."

"True, but things have changed. For example we're more attuned to diversity now."

"Two of the main characters were black, three if you count Preacher. They cursed in Mandarin."

The executive nodded. "Again, a good point, but we feel it sends ... the wrong message." The director looked confused, so he continued. "Let's start with the opening scene." He retrieved his notepad, found the correct page, and read the dialog.

"We meddle. People don't like to be meddled with. We tell them what to do, what to think. Don't run, don't walk. We're in their homes and in their heads and we haven't the right. We're meddlesome."

He dropped his notes on the desk with dramatic flourish. "You can see where this might conflict with some of the other entertainment being developed, yes?"

The director hesitated, sensing the fragility of the ice upon which he tread. "I'm sorry, sir, I just see a character being developed. The stage being set for conflict between two opposing forces that both believe they're in the right. Frankly, it's compelling cinema."

The executive exhaled, long and loud, through his nose while maintaining eye contact. "I'm not being clear. Gina, maybe you can add something here."

A smartly dressed woman in her fifties leaned forward on her elbows. "It's not a theme that resonates with the core fandom of the genre."

"But I go to all the big comic conferences every year. There's always a bunch of Firefly cosplayers. If anything, they're pretty intense."

The woman waved his comment aside. "Sure, but the *theme* of the movie doesn't agree with many of their core beliefs. We'd like to remove any cognitive dissonance they might feel." The young director was clearly skeptical. "Do you remember, late in the movie, when Captain Mal says," she donned reading glasses and dropped her eyes to the paper in front of her. "A year from now, ten, they'll swing back to the belief that they can make people better. And I do not hold to that." She removed her glasses and looked at the young man. "Obviously this isn't *offensive* per se, but it's not the kind of person we feel should be lionized."

"I see," said the director. "And you'd like to me ... massage the narrative."

"More bring it up to date," replied the first

executive. "In line with 2021 values."

The director nodded, and his mind processed the magnitude of the opportunity in front of him, as well as the cost to his artistic integrity.

"This sounds like a fascinating project. I can't wait to get started."

But I'm Not a Conservative!

"That's exactly what a conservative would say," said the young woman.

"But I'm not a conservative," replied the man. "I'm a lifelong Democrat."

"That doesn't mean anything. Many conservatives only vote Democratic because it suits them."

The man chewed on his lip and thought about that. It seemed silly that a conservative might vote against conservative candidates and measures, but, he wanted to be fair and hear the woman out. "If it suits them to vote Democrat, doesn't that imply they are not conservative? For example, I am pro-choice, within some constraints of course."

"You can be pro-choice and conservative."

"Okay, I'd like to see more renewable energy, and phase out coal and gas."

"What about nuclear?"

"It seems safe enough now. It should be part of an overall -"

"Conservative."

The man looked around for hidden cameras, but found none. No celebrities were pranking anyone today, at least not here. "Umm, I'd like to see capital gains taxes raised to match income tax. Wealth invested should not be prized above the work done by people without much to invest."

"So a wealth tax?"

"Well no, that's impractical to -"

"Conservative."

"I'd like to see a 'Marshall Plan' push in poor areas. There are a few things we know can improve outcomes. Couples counseling to encourage two-parent homes, for example. An end to many facets of the drug war. More skills-based training and free tutoring programs. I'd be happy to pay a little more in taxes to help."

The young woman nodded and studied him. "And would this 'Marshall Plan' be targeted by race, or class?"

"Class, naturally. The problem we need to solve isn't the color of someone's skin, it's their lack of opportunity, through no fault of their own."

"Conservative." She sipped her Cabernet.

"I'm not sure what else to say," the man protested. "I've been a liberal since before you were born."

The woman leaned across the table, skewering him with her intensity. "Gun control, yes or no."

"It depends on what you mean by gu-"

"Conservative. Trans rights, yes or no."

"Right to what? Transition? Be happy? Not be harassed? Of course!"

"What about compete in women's sports?"

"I don't know, that seems a little unfair."

"Bigot. And ..." Her hands flowered outward in a gesture of helplessness. "Conservative."

"Stop calling me a conservative!"

"I'd love to, dear, but it's simply the truth."

They both sat quietly for a minute, the woman smiling into her wine as she mentally replayed the drubbing she'd inflicted upon the man. Without preamble, the man pushed his chair away from the table and stood up.

"Where are you going?" she asked, watching him walk away.

He paused long enough to speak over one shoulder, while pointing to a boisterously blue collar table of folks sharing a pitcher of beer.

"I don't know what I am anymore, but I know I'd rather sit with them."

Fight the Mustache

On Monday there was only one of them. By Friday, they were legion.

It happened spontaneously, but not randomly. Sometimes it happened mid sentence, other times I'd glance away from someone, and when I glanced back, there he was. Hitler.

I didn't understand how it was possible. At first I doubted my lived experience, even going so far as to ask around on social media. It turned out it wasn't all that uncommon after all. Across the English-speaking world, enlightened people reported being surrounded by Hitlers.

The first time it happened, I'd just enunciated my disappointment in California voters for, yet again, rejecting racial preferences in college admissions. A man - it was *always* a man - chimed in with his unrequested view - it was *always* unrequested - that he voted against them, and felt that any special considerations should focus more on wealth than skin color.

BAM! Hitler.

Later that day in the break room, I was explaining the racism inherent in climate change. A coworker replied - again, unrequested - that I had a point about the effects hitting people of color harder than white people, but she thought it was an accidental byproduct and, had industrialization begun near the equator, we'd be seeing the exact same phenomenon in reverse.

Hitler.

Worse, it started happening to people I hadn't even engaged. Minus even the typical Hitlerian pronouncement of their voting preference, or personal beliefs, people were morphing into Hitler. Outside work, I hailed a cab. The driver pulled to the curb ahead of me, where a man hopped in, leaving me stranded.

Pop! Pop! Two Hitlers.

A staff meeting, where my supervisor assured me he'd "get to" the equity curriculum I'd spent hours drafting, and not a single colleague pressed the issue on my behalf.

Hitlers. All of them.

By Friday morning, I was scared to go to work. Not only were most of my coworkers sporting tiny Lego mustaches and shouting at me in German, many of the people I recognized on my commute were too. The final straw came when I watched a bus thunder past. The billboard, a seemingly benign photograph of two beautiful twenty somethings who'd ostensibly met on the dating app mentioned above them, transformed *while I watched.*

I ran the rest of the way home, slamming the door and leaning against it. Once I recovered my breath, I dragged the refrigerator in front of the door. I'd find an extension cord later.

Sobbing, I called my mother. She was aghast to learn Hitlers were graduating from ubiquitous to universal. It was then my father joined the call. His views on the capital gains tax slammed into me, and his voice changed. He was suddenly younger, angrily barking at me in German. I screamed and hung up.

The room spun. My back found the refrigerator, and I sank to the floor as my vision narrowed. The last thought I had, as the poster in my hallway morphed to Hitler, a single fist raised in triumph while the other gripped a microphone was, *"I see a little silhouetto of a Hitler ..."*

Ugly

A young girl failed her math test. Her parents were quite sore.

"No more television on school days," they said, "and its a tutor for you!"

And so the girl toiled. Some days, her tutor helped her. Other days her father did his best. Many were the days she cried in frustration. Many were the days she wanted to rage, to throw her book and scream, "I can't do this! I quit!"

But she never did.

As the months pressed on, the girl acclimated to her schedule. She grew accustomed to not understanding at first, and expected to struggle to succeed.

But succeed she did.

The girl began to understand she was capable. Powerful. Soon she repeated this pattern with her many subjects, and though she was not the smartest child in her class, she placed near the top of it on every exam. With this habit, the girl began tutoring other students.

When it came time for college, the girl was courted by many universities, and to the Ivy Leagues she went. There she learned of her privilege. She was confused again, as she suspected she had many privileges, but was tutored again until she recognized that only one mattered. Thus the girl focused on that, attending rallies, and penning the most scathing of opinion pieces for the school paper.

The girl's habits changed. Knowing now that her acceptance to multiple Ivy League institutions had less to do with her studious nature, and more to do with immutable traits she had not earned or wanted, she spent her study time organizing and protesting. It was then she noticed her eyes. Had they subtly shifted? One seemed lower than the other. She asked her friends, who assured her she was unchanged.

More rallies needed organizing, for the Ivy Leagues were a bastion of suffering and intolerance. Thus was the girl kept busy. Math, long her favorite subject, felt so distant. The distance gnawed at her, but knowing she put the same meager efforts toward her social science courses and was earning high marks convinced her the professor might be threatened by high achieving women. She endeavored to investigate his social media posts.

Only she grew distracted again by her appearance. This time it was her mouth that seemed just a touch amiss, with one corner noticeably higher than the other. Having only just grown accustomed to her new eyes, the effect was quite disconcerting.

But her friends assured her anew that she looked the same as the prior day, and the prior week. Wondering if she might need to see a female identifying, BIPOC physician, the girl focused on bringing social change to the warped chasm of bigotry that was her university.

Midterms came, and the girl was shocked to receive her first F since grade school. Her friends were ever so supportive, co-signing the complaint against her math professor. He quickly issued a public apology and admitted she had truly earned a B.

Despite her professor collecting his salary while on suspension, the girl was happy at her achievement. Until she noticed that the left side of her head was bald. How and when such calamity struck, she hadn't the faintest idea, but she was truly panicked. On top of her deformities (she inwardly chastised herself, knowing that somehow that word was offensive), the next week she would see her parents for the first time in months. What would they think? What would they say?

Anxiety and broken sleep left the girl muddled, and her parents noticed immediately. What they *didn't* notice was her enormous bald spot, her misshapen mouth, or her uneven eyes.

"Come inside." Her mother wrapped a loving arm over her shoulder. "I'll make you your favorite soup."

Wondering how she'd manage to eat it without making a fool of herself, she let herself be guided and doted upon. On the table lay her father's copy of Stephen Hawking's "A Brief History of Time." Absentmindedly, the girl pulled the marked up, dog-eared book to her, picked a chapter, and began reading. Her mother served the soup, but, seeing her daughter's familiar study frown, quietly left the girl to read.

An hour passed, and the girl realized her soup had gone cold. She felt a little tired, but it was a different sort of tired. The kind of tired one *earns* by focusing on a difficult task. The girl smiled as she placed the soup in the microwave. She shut the door, catching her reflection in the polished surface.

The girl's deformities had disappeared.

A Thrilling Conclusion

Sally dyed her hair, and no one cared.

Thinking she'd chosen the wrong color, she picked the brightest shades of pink, purple, and blue she could find, and tried again. But no one cared.

Sally was confused, so she pierced one nostril. Her parents cared, but that was all.

Bereft of guidance, Sally invested upwards of two hours watching videos on social media, that she might know herself. With her deeper understanding of both her needs and the world's, Sally found herself a boyfriend. Yet no one cared. Outside of her family, close friends, and, naturally, her boyfriend, no one cared.

Thus Sally got a girlfriend too. Now people began to care. Her family made some attempts at being supportive, but was a touch confused. Her friends congratulated her. Her boyfriend thought he loved the idea, though he soon left her. But Sally gained hundreds of followers on social media. Weeks passed, and Sally's audience grew with every online lecture she produced. Until Sally plateaued.

Each new lecture garnered fewer 'likes' than the previous one, and Sally's anxiety grew in proportion to her online momentum. Comments such as, "these are all the same," and, "LOL yer dum," detonated against her self worth. So Sally did the only rational thing - she discovered she was really a man.

This time many people cared. Not just her baffled

and bigoted parents, who suggested she might be going through a phase. Not just her close friends, who'd been rather less close of late. And not just her girlfriend, who announced she was, herself, gender fluid, thus romantically unconcerned by the news.

Sally was born again, as Sal. Sal was an online sensation, and his followers grew to the tens of thousands, with many cheering his bravery. Sal released new content every week, and thought he was on the path to his dream job of being a social media influencer. A soap company contacted him, offering to pay for a sponsored post.

But Sal ran out of ideas for content rather quickly. Worse, so many young women emulated his success that he went from extraordinary to really quite ordinary. Sal knew what he had to do, and scheduled his double mastectomy. To the accolades of his online fans, Sal removed the most obvious vestiges of his former self. His 'likes' and 'shares' skyrocketed again, as did praise for his heroic struggle against the society that was so clearly intent on oppressing him.

It was during a routine post-operation visit that Sal bumped into the mother of his former best friend, who he'd lost contact with during his rise to stardom.

"Doctor Winston," he stood, and greeted her. "I didn't realize you worked here. How is Jenn? We haven't talked in forever, I feel awful."

"Jennifer's fine, thank you." She examined Sal's chart. "She's pre-med now."

For some reason, Sal felt the urge to squirm. "Well, you see what I've been doing," he joked.

"Yes." Doctor Winston set the notes down and looked at him. "You've become a boring young man."

Intro to Neo-Pronouns

Darren was excited for his first college party. He grew up in a small, unremarkable town, and in some ways felt small and unremarkable himself, so he made sure the party was of the small and unremarkable variety, that he might fit in.

Come half past nine, he knocked on the door of a cute little house with a well-tended flowerbed. A young woman answered, and he introduced himself. "Hi, I'm Darren. Kathy invited me. Is she here yet?"

The young woman sized him up before answering. "*She* is not. *They* is."

Darren stood on the porch, feeling rather dumb. "I'm sorry?"

"Kathy's pronouns are they/them."

"Oh, I'm sorry, I hadn't thought to ask. They/them it is." He grinned, and the as-yet unnamed young woman let him pass. He'd read about personal pronouns, and thought the idea long overdue. No one in his high school had used a personal pronoun, but then, his high school was small, and unremarkable.

"Darren!" bellowed a voice.

He saw a hand wave across the room and strode toward it. "Kathy, hi. Thanks again for inviting me. I've only met the woman at the door, and I didn't catch her name."

Kathy frowned. "That's Melinda, and *she's* a *fae*."

"A ... fae." It took him a moment, but Darren's mind caught up to his mouth, and he closed it, nodding to buy more time. "Okay, that's cool." He cringed, feeling quite provincial, but Kathy pretended not to notice.

She leaned toward him and lowered her voice. "My friend asked who you were when you walked in." Kathy nodded to a pretty young woman in the kitchen. "Would you like to meet ver?"

"Ver?" He shook his head. "Right! Yeah. Ver. Got it." He was starting to get the hang of college parties, and admitted they were exciting, though he hadn't expected them to be this confusing.

Ignoring his clumsy recovery, Kathy led on, until they (plural) shared a circle with their (singular) friend. "Katie, this is Darren. He/Him. Darren, meet Katie."

Darren smiled and shook Katie's hand, both exhilarated at meeting a woman with such beautiful blue hair, and a tad apprehensive at her name.

Kathy, they.
Katie, ve.
I got this.[5]

As the conversation flowed, Darren grew fonder of Katie, and he felt ver warming to him in kind. Then, a handsome young man with an easy charm approached.

---

[5] By the third name, I had to write this crap out to keep it straight.

Scary Stories to Tell the Woke in the Dark

"Hey all!" He placed a six pack of beer on the counter beside them (plural). "Who's the new person?" He produced a flawless smile and a hand for Darren to ingest. "I'm Chad. Sorry about the name, I promise I'm not horrible."

The circle laughed, including Darren, though he had no idea why.

Darren introduced himself and made small talk, but as he was working on his third drink, and Chad hadn't thought to mention his(?) pronouns, Darren found himself loathe to engage him(?).

Against his better judgment, Darren drank that beer, then one more. Though their (plural) customs seemed bizarrely intricate, his new friends were warm and genial. Enough so that he was utterly relaxed when Melinda approached with faer boyfriend. Or girlfriend. Darren was unsure, so he kept quiet.

The circle laughed and exchanged stories about high school mischief, and Darren's timidity receded. Until disaster struck.

It happened as he recounted the moment his parents saw the tattoo he'd snuck off and gotten on his eighteenth birthday. "I can't show it to you now," he said, laughing, "but it looks a lot like hers." He pointed to Melinda's forearm, which was covered with an intricate, Celtic-looking design.

The group froze, and Darren realized what he'd done.

"Oh, I'm *so* sorry, Melinda." He felt the blood in his cheeks, and searched the faces of his new friends for forgiveness. They (plural) suddenly found something interesting to stare at, on the walls, the ceiling ... "It's the beer." Darren put his drink on the counter. "I guess I hit my limit." He tried to break the tension with a chuckle.

Melinda was visibly shaken, but nodded at him. "It's okay, I know you're trying."

The group exhaled, and the night continued. Until Darren's second faux pas.

"Looks like Chad's on his last beer," he laughed, as Chad stumbled out of the bathroom toward them. The levity died. "What? What's wrong?"

"Chad goes by xe/xer," said Kathy.

"Woah, he ... *xe* never mentioned that."

"Did you think to ask xem?" said Kathy.

Darren admitted the thought hadn't occurred to him, and apologized. Still buzzed, and now thoroughly flustered, he spent the next hour politely laughing, but only speaking in terse replies when asked direct questions. Eventually, he bade the group farewell and returned to his dorm.

"What was with Darren?" asked Katie. "He didn't say more than ten words in the last hour."

"Got me," said Kathy. "I barely know him." They (singular) tapped their (singular) chin. "I wonder if he's racist[6]."

---

[6] This was a fun one to spellcheck.

Imagination

The gate always took so long to open. Impatiently, I stabbed the remote control button a few more times, knowing it wouldn't make any difference. It was my own fault for not calling ahead and having one of the au pairs open it ahead of time.

Brushing it off, I pulled into the roundabout and saw two cars in the visitor area. The sprinklers were on, dousing both the landscape and my mood with cold water. Late as I was, there was no chance I'd skip hair and makeup before a shoot, even one as trivial as this.

I parked and dialed my stylist as I speed walked to the front door.

"Sarah, I ... hold on." I hurried past the obnoxiously loud fountain. Stupid thing, it was past time to get rid of it. "I'm heading up now. Tell ... whats-her-face you'll both need to work on me at the same time."

"Francine," said Sarah.

"What?" It took my brain a second to catch up. "Whatever."

I reached the door and pounded on it while rescuing my feet from the medieval devices I'd had strapped to them the last few hours. The butler answered and I pushed past, handing him my shoes. I raced up the stairs before remembering that pantyhose don't grip marble, thus was my good deed for the day nearly derailed by a broken neck.

Spent and panting from the various ordeals, I burst into my home studio, shouting instructions and snapping my fingers. Knowing time was far from an ally, I hopped into the makeup chair, only to have my key FOB fall from my pocket and shatter on the floor.

"Damn these stupid FOBs," I spat. "That's the last Lexus I buy until they make keys that don't explode at the slightest touch."

Fortunately my assistant was on hand with a cappuccino and the spare FOB. Seeing my harried state, she intercepted at least two interruptions, proving that good help is hard, but not impossible, to find.

"Remember," I told the room, "make me look good, but not *too* good. This is us connecting with people stuck in quarantine."

Finally, after forever in the chair, I felt human enough to face the camera. I strode across the studio, where we'd be filming, and took a moment to practice mindfulness. The crew was ready. I was ready.

"Okay, take one, in three … two … one …" The director gestured, it was 'go time.'

Taking a beat to marry my inner to my outer voice, I let Gaia use me as her vessel, and peace washed through me.

"Imagine there's no heaven …"[7]

"Perfect," said the director. "That's a wrap, we'll

---

[7] Web Search: "celebrity imagine"

polish it in post."

The Scorpion and the Frog, 2021

A scorpion wanted to cross the river ahead, so it bade the frog help.

"Please, Mister Frog, will you carry me across the river?" it asked.

"No," the frog replied, "if I carry you across the river, you'll sting me and we'll drown."

"I would not do that, for then *both* of us would drown."

The frog squinted at the scorpion, as if considering its words. "No, I do not think I will."

"But -"

"No buts," interrupted the frog. "I've seen you sting every frog in every direction. You're a complete disaster. Now get the hell away from me."

With that, the frog hopped across the river, and lived a long, happy life[8].

---

[8] Web Search: "scorpion and frog"

Must be Nice

The boy needed money, so he bagged groceries after school.

One day, not long after the boy started, a man of perhaps fifty visited the store and requested help loading groceries into his car. Tired and gruff from a long day, the boy was obliged to help him, and smile while doing it. The boy eyed the older man the whole time.

There's nothing wrong with him. And look at this fancy car. I can't stand these trust fund babies.

But outwardly, the boy smiled. Until the end, when the man slowly slid into the driver's seat, and handed the boy a dollar for his help. The boy stared at the bill, then at the man, then at the car.

"Must be nice." He said.

The man chuckled, and drove away.

The boy's life moved on. He worked at the grocery store all through high school, as cashier, stocker, supervisor, book keeper, and finally, in his twenties, manager. As the owner aged, he sold a stake of the store to the boy, now a man. Eventually, the owner retired, and sold the entire store to the man.

The store did well, and so did the town surrounding the store. It grew and grew, and the man opened a second store. Soon he opened a third store, and a fourth. By the man's fortieth birthday, he owned and operated a chain of stores.

But the man was lonely.

While his business thrived, the man wondered if there was nothing else to life. As he approached his forty-fifth birthday, he decided he was done. With little trouble, he found a buyer, retired from the grocery business, and moved to a small town near the beach. He'd always wanted to live near the beach.

The man needed a few weeks to relax. To tamp down the guilt from not being at work twelve hours a day. But over time he ventured out to enjoy each sunny day. Eventually, he even went to a nice restaurant with a bar, that he might meet people.

It was there the man handed his keys to a young valet, and heard the forgotten words.

"Must be nice."

The Sleepy Dog

There once was a giant dog. It was a tired dog.

As the dog settled down to sleep, a crowd of noisy people approached. The crowd stopped near the dog and argued quite heatedly.

Grumpy at the noise, the dog got up and approached the crowd. "What is this all about? Can you not see I'm trying to sleep?"

"It's his fault," said the loudest fellow, pointing to an elderly man. "He is quite the miscreant, and all this bedlam is his doing. If you'd eat him, you'd have your quiet."

The dog, in no mood to bicker, promptly gobbled up the elderly man and returned to bed. He settled in, but was soon roused by more shouting.

"I'm so tired," the dog told the crowd. "Can you not do this elsewhere?"

The same fellow pointed to a middle-aged woman. "This intolerant woman is stirring up trouble. Eat her and you can sleep."

The dog was suspicious, but swallowed the woman. The crowd quieted, and the dog was quick to fall asleep again, though he swore he heard a man and a woman politely discussing tea in the distance.

It wasn't long before another commotion forced the exhausted beast from bed. "What now?" he asked the noisy fellow.

The noisy fellow pointed to a young man. "That is the man you want. His views are quite problematic, and he stirs up trouble everywhere he goes."

Suspicious, the dog pretended to eat the man before laying back down in bed. It let the man crawl from his mouth, but warned him to silence while they watched the crowd. Soon the noisy fellow was quarreling yet again, this time with a child about the moral implications of her stuffed toy.

The dog had seen enough. With a snarl, it charged the man and swallowed him whole. The crowd thanked the dog and promised there would be no more disturbances.

Sparing them a crabby look, the dog curled up in his bed. "Finally I can get some rest."

As the dog drifted to sleep, an argument erupted. The dog sprang from bed, ready to eat every last person in the crowd. But they were all sitting peacefully, enjoying each other's company in low voices.

"I don't understand," murmured the dog. But then it recognized the noisy fellow's voice and peered at its stomach.

The dog understood. And it wept.

The Superstition of Elders

"I'm just saying there's got to be a better way to do it," said the first doctor. "It feels silly deciding like this, when our grandparents, and everyone before them, knew the answer instinctively."

"Careful." The second doctor looked around. They were alone. "You've been talking like this more lately. People are noticing."

"I don't care!"

The second doctor blanched, then power walked to the door and eased it shut, hoping no one would ask why. "So how *should* we decide?"

"We should ... I don't know." He thought about the vintage midwife's diary his father had given him upon graduating medical school. He'd thumbed through it a few times out of curiosity. "We could see if it has a penis or a vagina."

His colleague frowned. "That's a little primitive, doctor. You know there are people with both, or neither, or improp ..." She caught herself. "Differently formed genitalia that don't conform to Bronze Age superstitions."

He conceded with a nod. "Maybe we can check for chromosomes. If it has XY, we assign it 'male,' if XX, 'female.'"

"Chromosomes dictate genitalia. All you've done is move a step upstream. I'm sorry doctor, it's just unreliable pseudo science."

Scary Stories to Tell the Woke in the Dark

"I'm not so sure," he replied. "We've been doing this for years. How many babies have you seen that weren't obviously 'A' or 'B'? Maybe we're over thinking this."

The second doctor leaned over the newborn to hiss at him. "Now you're being phobic. I need you to stop."

"Phobic of *what*? We don't even have words for these ... these ... conditions anymore." He saw her bristling. "Hear me out. What if we let the genitalia guide us in most cases, and when it wasn't clear, we treat the child on a case-by-base basis, with love and compassion?"

Her eyes softened at the mention of love and compassion. "What you speak of is heresy," she whispered. "Even if I agreed, and I'm not saying I do, your license would be revoked the first time you contradicted the official decision."

"What if there wasn't one? What if we 'forgot' to follow the process?"

"You know there's an audit trail. You'd be caught the same day. This is madness, doctor. Let it go."

The first doctor withered under the bombardment of her medical realpolitik, and soon stood across from her, a defeated man.

"For what it's worth, I'm sorry. But we really do need to finish processing this child."

He nodded and helped her roll the crib to the machine in the corner. She pushed the over sized red button, watching as a slot in the back of the machine opened to release a coin. The coin rolled down a deep groove in the giant metal thumb to rest on the thumbnail. The thumb slowly lowered, then jerked up, causing the coin to spin through the air before landing on the tray before them[9].

"Well there you go," said the second doctor, "it's a boy. See? All that anxiety over nothing." They wheeled the boy back to his spot in the nursery. "Does it strike you as sexist that it's 'heads' for boys and 'tails' for girls?"

---

[9] Web Search: "cnn no consensus assigning sex"

Another Great Day

A boy was late for school.

"Hurry up," his birthing person cried from the front door. "And don't forget your glasses this time!"

The boy shuddered as memories of yesterday rushed back to him. He'd forgotten his glasses yesterday. Grabbing them, he sighed in relief, and donned them before running to the car.

"Are your ear pieces in?" his birthing person asked, raising a knowing eyebrow.

He gave a sheepish smile, feeling the earbuds bump gently against his cheeks as they dangled from the frames. He tucked them into his ears and got into the car.

"I hope you finished your homework this morning," the boy heard his parent's muffled voice say. He frowned and tapped the earbuds. A soft melody began to play. The voice no longer troubled him.

The parent stopped speaking, and the music stopped. They finished the ride in silence.

"Love you, have a great day!" The parent waved goodbye as they pulled away from the curb.

"Hi Billy," came a voice.

The boy turned to see Veronica, one of his best friends, approaching with a smile. She was wearing her bright yellow shirt again. The one with the entire logo or pattern blurred out. He'd meant to ask her what was on it for some time. They walked to class together.

"Did you do the assign-" began Veronica.

"Siiiingin' in the rain, just siiiiingin' in the raaaaain."

Billy smiled. He'd always enjoyed this song. He nodded at his friend until she stopped talking.

History was his favorite class. It was just the right blend of instruction and music, unlike math, which seemed unnecessary, as it was nothing more than one long concert.

"Billy, what happened in 1812?"

He thought a bit. "The Civil War?"

His teacher's eyebrows became blurry, indicating a frown. "No Billy, that was -"

"The hills are alive ... with the sound of music. With songs they have sung ... for a thousand yeeeeears ..."

Billy's teacher sighed and moved on.

The day progressed much like any other, and Billy's birthing parent was waiting for him after school. "How was your day, honey?"

"Great. Just like every other day."

The First

Peter was the first. Or at least he *thought* he was. He didn't really care, but it seemed important to a lot of people.

A Hispanic man had never been appointed to his position before, and he helped celebrate the progress it implied. Until a random stranger on the internet dredged up a picture of another Hispanic man in his position, two decades prior.

Fortunately, Peter was gay, and was thus the first gay man appointed to his position. Except he wasn't. A bit of digging uncovered a gay predecessor, and that upset a surprising number of people.

"Well," one said, "was the gay predecessor Hispanic?"

It turned out he was, but several hard-hitting reporters saw the value of combining identities. Peter, for his part, was busy at his new job, but agreed to an interview with one such plucky young lady.

"Do you identify as a woman?" the reporter asked.

Peter glanced down at his hairy arms, his tie, and the photograph on his desk of him in his college football uniform. "No, can't say I do."

She seemed disappointed. "Gender fluid?"

"I don't follow."

"Never mind." She waved the thought aside. "I don't suppose you're vegan."

"No, I avoid most meat because heart disease runs in my family. I still eat fish though."

"Aha!" She scribbled some notes. "This may sound forward, but how many partners do you have? Please, feel free to not answer if this offends you."

Peter snorted. "I've been with the same partner for seven years. We're really quite boring, sorry."

"Hmmm. Did you feel an immediate connection? Was the relationship hot and steamy for a while and then settled into something more ... stable?"

"Not really. I was never comfortable with the hook-up scene. We took our time and got to know each other."

Her mood brightened. "So you'd say you have to really connect with someone on an emotional level before things become intimate?"

"That's pretty accurate. I'm also more attracted to people's brains than their looks. Don't get me wrong, I appreciate a stunner just like anyone else, but a clever mind is huge for me." A gentle notification sounded from his computer speaker, causing him to squint at his monitor. "Look, I'm sorry, but I have a lot of work to do."

"Sure, sure. One more question. Have you taken a genetic ancestry test?"

"Actually yes. Hold on." Peter clicked and typed for a minute. "Here we go. Turns out I have a great-

great-grandmother from Haiti, or thereabouts. Who knew?" He spun his monitor to face the reporter.

She studied the graph before asking for a printout. Peter, not seeing what harm might come from such benign information, agreed, and she left his office with a spring in her step.

The next morning, Peter's husband called just as he'd sat down behind his desk. "Congratulations!"

"For what?"

"Don't play dumb."

"I honestly have no idea what you're talking about," said Peter, though he suspected the strange young woman who interviewed him the previous day was somehow involved.

His husband sighed. "Congratulations on being the first gay, pescatarian, demisexual, sapiosexual, Hispanic/African American of Caribbean descent to be appointed to your position!"

The Balloon

There once was a little yellow balloon. It began life tied to a tiny weight. But it thought the weight was a silly idea, so it began to work itself loose.

The knot was tight, and the twine was strong, so the little yellow balloon strained and strained to no avail. But soon, after much effort, it freed itself of the silly weight, and floated up, up, and up some more.

"Look at me," it called to the other balloons. "I have ascended, while the rest of you huddle near the ground, stuck to your foolish weights."

"Come back," the other balloons cried. "Without your weight you'll be carried to and fro, at the mercy of every gust of wind!"

The little yellow balloon just laughed. So simple were the others. So crude. It floated higher and higher, and as it did, the wind blew stronger and stronger. So strong that the little yellow balloon got scared.

"Maybe the others were right," whispered a faint voice.

"No!" it shouted as a particularly nasty burst of wind carried it away. "This is where I wanted to go." And the little yellow balloon spoke with such force that it started to believe just that. However, the wind pushed it into an ugly land. A land of sharp rocks, and cacti. Still the little yellow balloon shouted to all who would listen, "This is the way! Everybody look at me!"

But everybody looked at it, and they were not impressed.

"Look at that stupid balloon," laughed a salamander. "It has no idea what it's doing."

"I hope it comes closer," hissed a rattlesnake.

"That balloon used to be funny, now it just screams in a manic appeal for attention," said a passing hawk.

That was when the little yellow balloon knew it was in a bad place. The faint voice whispered again. "You've lost your way, little balloon." The little yellow balloon started to wonder if it had made a terrible mistake[10], when suddenly, the wind shifted. It blew and blew, in the opposite direction, and carried the little yellow balloon back the way it came.

Soon the little yellow balloon saw the balloons it left behind. While it had flown so very far in the wind, the others had drifted only so far as their weights and twine permitted. Now that the wind had reversed itself, they too were driven the other way. But again, only as far as their weights and twine allowed. As its anchored kin fluttered below, the little yellow balloon zoomed past, cackling in triumph.

This time, the other balloons did not bother to shout warnings or advice. They knew the little yellow balloon was headed out to sea, but they were tired of being talked down to.

They no longer cared.

10[10] Web Search: "chelsea handler vogue cuomo first lady"

A Simple Lesson

The Professor stopped the music. "Who can tell me what's wrong with that song?"

No one raised their hand. No one but Becky.

"The first word, for starters. It's non-inclusive and insensitive to birthing people who don't identify as female. Who says 'mama' anymore anyway?"

Leonard raised his hand. "What's a 'birthing person.' Isn't that just a weird way of saying 'mom?'"

"We'll not have that talk in here, Leonard," said the Professor. "Becky, please continue."

"She's also helping her son, who, from the singer's voice, sounds white. How many songs do we need about the problems of white men?"

The Professor nodded, gesturing for more.

"The part about finding a woman to love is overtly heteronormative. This 'mother,'" Becky made air quotes around the word, "has no idea if her son is straight, or even how he self identifies."

Leonard couldn't help himself, and blurted, "I'm so lost. All that's happened is a mother told her son that he'll fall in love with a woman when he's older." He felt twenty or more eyes fling hostility at him.

"Your confusion is noted," said the Professor, scratching something in his notebook.

"The line about 'someone up above' is also offensive," said Becky. "Not everyone believes in God, or just one god." She side-eyed Leonard.

"What about the part where she tells her son to mind his soul, instead of chasing someone else's gold?" asked Leonard. "That sounds like great advice!"

"Yes, but why did it have to be a rich *man's* gold she warned him about? The implication is wealth resides with men. Then there's the casual racism."

Leonard's nearly leapt from his seat. "Racism! It's a mom giving her son advice. The song doesn't even mention race!"

"Well, first of all, the line about troubles just 'passing' demonstrates a galling degree of white male privilege." She looked to the Professor, who nodded. "But the tone of the song implies a yearning for a simpler past. When things were better, because white men owned and controlled everything."

"How did you get all that from what he sang?" Leonard leaned forward in his chair and stared at Becky. "Are you okay?"

"Professor, I'm feeling unsafe right now," answered Becky.

"Un-what?"

The Professor left his white board to stand between the two. "Leonard, I'm afraid you're going to have to leave."

Leonard crammed his book into his backpack and

stood up. "You all are crazy. I'm going to the office right now to drop this class."

The class watched him storm from the room, silent until a young woman from the last row spoke.

"I should make sure he gets there. You know, without causing any trouble."

"That's very noble of you, Miranda. Please, be careful."

"Yes, Professor."

Miranda left, and the class resumed arguing. After an exhausting hour, the students had worked themselves into a rage, and they left spent, yet simmering with bitterness.

Across campus, on a sunny hill, Leonard and Miranda shared a sandwich[11].

11[11] Youtube search: "a simple man lyrics"

The Swinging Door

I do not understand
in this awakened age
why I am banned
for being but a sage

> Ah, a sage you may be
> but only to some
> and not to me

Thus I am silenced
ostracized, cast out
Why not refute me
with the wisdom you tout?

> Engagement is hard
> so very distressing
> Why bother?
> Your views are upsetting

Are you really so fragile
so close to the verge
that your world view might crumble
with scarcely an urge?

> I stand for justice
> you stand for hate
> no more need be said
> to decide your fate

So incredibly unfair
that slant, that distortion
I'm a human being, not a villain
of comic book proportion

Though your point is valid
it offers no protection
I'm only applying *your* rules
You lost the election

The Just Plain Weird

Assault on Jupiter

"An unknown vessel dropped out of light speed just over a million kilometers from Jupiter station, Captain."

The ship appeared on sensors, banking wildly to avoid being an easy target for human gunners before it got its bearings.

"Red alert, open a channel," said Captain Milano. He steered his light cruiser toward the ship and pushed the bar his left hand rested on forward as far as it would go. The deep churning of the engine grew, making conversation difficult, but not impossible. *The Matriarchy* accelerated to its top speed of two thousand clicks per second, and he eased the throttle back, letting it coast toward their target.

"They're ignoring us, sir," said his comms officer, Lieutenant Sheffield. "Should I fire a spread of jammers?"

"Should you *what*, Lieutenant?" ask the captain.

"Sorry sir, should I *release* a spread of jammers?"

"That's better. And yes, please do."

Sheffield launched the probes, which sped from *The Matriarchy* in every direction, jamming every frequency but the tiny band used by The Alliance.

"Alien vessel targeted, sir," said Lieutenant Jackson. "Firing on your order."

"Oh. Emm. Gee." Milano stood up and walked to Jackson's station, where he glared down at him, hands on his hips. "Care to repeat that, Lieutenant?"

Jackson paled. "My apologies, sir. Still acclimating I guess." He stopped stammering to consider his words. "Foreign vess -"

"Try again," interrupted Milano.

"*Undocumented* vessel targeted, sir." He self consciously wiped the sweat from his forehead and looked up at the captain. "Um, sending ... negative ... energy toward them when you say to?"

"Clumsy, but acceptable." Captain Milano returned to his station in time to see a cluster of missiles impact against the forward shields. He banked to avoid the next salvo. "Lieutenant Jackson, *disinvite* them."

Jackson fired the forward particle beams. "A hit, sir, no effect."

"A *connection*, Lieutenant," warned the captain.

"Yes, sir, a connection. No effect."

"Another missile salvo launched, launching countermeasures," yelled Sheffield. She cringed in anticipation of the rebuke.

The void between ships filled with tracers and chaff as Milano considered whether 'launch' was problematic. "Very good, Lieutenant."

"Another connection, sir," said Jackson. "Our

energy weap ... our energy thingies aren't damag ... aren't causing physical ... discomfort for them."

"Contact Jupiter station, rainbow alert."

Sheffield shrank from the order. "Sir! Backup is minutes away. Shouldn't we -"

"No time, Lieutenant. We need to evacuate all people of color, trans people, and, time permitting, gay people. Send that alert, now."

"What about Asians and Jewish people," asked Sheffield.

Milano, suddenly engrossed in piloting the cruiser, didn't answer.

"Alert sent, sir. Another alie ... unknown vessel just dropped into local space!"

In that moment, Captain Milano understood what he had to do. "Prepare the Guevara Cannon."

"Yes sir," answered Jackson, a quiver betraying his dread of the experimental weapon. "Weapon charging. Ready in thirty seconds." He touched his forehead, his heart, and each shoulder, in the outlawed pattern he'd seen his grandmother use. He wasn't sure what it meant, but if it was in any way asking the universe for luck, it was worth the month in jail.

Milano weaved and banked the cruiser, trailing plasma from the shields as missiles continued to strike the ship. Shield strength had plummeted to seventeen percent when the Guevara Cannon timer hit zero. With a quick jerk on the starboard thrusters, and a matching move on the steering stick, Milano sent *The Matriarch* into a controlled spin long enough to point its nose at the ships chasing them.

"Connect!"

A rumble shook them to their cores, and a burst of invisible energy turned both enemy ships to dust.

"A hit, sir!" shouted Jackson, too excited to recognize the inherent violence of his speech. "Both ships destroyed!"

The Captain opened his mouth to reply, when the rumble began anew. "Shut the Guevara Cannon down, Lieutenant, that's an order."

"I did, sir. There must be some kind of malfunction … Goddess no." He turned to the Captain. "It's targeting our reinforcements."

"Shut it down, now!"

"I can't!"

The cannon discharged again, atomizing a pair of Alliance heavy cruisers. The rumble immediate started to build again.

"It's targeting the Jupiter station, Captain. I can't shut it down."

"Sir," said Sheffield in a tiny voice, "sir, we have to self destruct. It's the three of us, or the thousands of people on that research outpost."

"What? No!" said Milano. "It wouldn't really destroy all those people. I'm sure it's run its course.

But just in case, we should probably head to the escape pods."

The Least Dangerous Game

Ralph landed their shuttle in an abandoned amusement park outside the city. The stealth modules hid it from prying eyes, and Cal volunteered to stay behind to 'handle' anyone that somehow sniffed it out. Ralph was still a little suspicious about how quickly he'd volunteered, and could have sworn he'd seen a smirk before doing a double take.

"Okay then, good luck you two. Let me know if you … ya know, need anything." Cal waved from the top of the ramp as it rose, sealing the ship and erasing the only visible slice of it.

Albert checked the power level on his energy cannon. "He seems chipper."

"Yeah. I don't like it."

With nothing for it, they activated their personal stealth systems and set a brisk pace into the city. It'd been decades since their last hunting trip to this part of Earth the locals referred to as 'America,' and they were jazzed to see what new toys these humans had dreamed up.

"Hold up," said Ralph. He leaned against a brick facade to catch his breath, blurting out the first question he thought of to cover his panting. "You think we should head into the city proper again, or start with something on the outskirts?" He pinched his belly fat and frowned.

Albert pretended not to notice. "I'm loose. There used to be a lot of gangs a little east of downtown, let's check there first."

They jogged, slower this time, eastward, taking care to avoid bumping into the smaller humans.

"I don't get it," said Albert after several minutes. "This used to be a pretty rough area."

Ralph shrugged. "Maybe they're finally getting their act together. It was bound to happen."

"I'm not so sure. Something doesn't feel right. Let's hang out …" he searched the area, settling on a second-story balcony above a busy liquor store, "there."

They eyed the flimsy ladder to the balcony. Prudence dictated they come through the apartment window.

The balcony creaked a few minutes later, as Albert followed Ralph out the window.

"Careful now," said Ralph.

"Right, *I'm* the problem here," muttered Albert.

"What?"

"Hmm? Nothing. Hey, there's a fight. Look, a mob is forming."

They quieted and watched, eager for the trip's first taste of violence.

"Wait, what's going on?" asked Ralph. "Is that mob … are they scolding him?"

"I think so. I can only make out half the words, but it sounds like ... what's a 'microaggression?'"

"Got me. Why is everyone snapping their fingers at that guy?" Ralph turned to Albert. "I forget, does this species have telekinesis?"

"Nah, you're thinking of *Merth*, this is *Earth*. Oh god, is that guy *crying*?"

"I've seen enough. Whatever's happening here, we're not allowed to kill any of these people."

As they stood up to leave, a bolt popped out of the wall behind them, and the balcony sagged.

"Oh sh-"

They tumbled below, crushing the mob under visible steel and invisible flesh.

"Dude, we're in so much trouble. Run!" Ralph sprinted away, Albert on his heels.

●

By the time they stopped, they were outside a police station.

"This might work," said Albert. "Let's listen, follow their law enforcement. *They'll* dig up some dangerous types we can get after."

With no better ideas, Ralph agreed, and they settled in. Soon, three pairs of police officers ran to their cars, and, with the two hunters in tow, sped toward what could only be a catastrophe.

"Where is everyone?" Albert panted as they fought to keep pace with the squad cars. "I remember there being a lot more people walking around last - woops!" He accidentally shoulder checked a young man riding an electric scooter on the sidewalk. "Sorry!" There was no indication the jumbled heap of flesh and scooter heard or understood him.

They rounded a corner to see the squad cars parked at different angles, the officers taking cover behind their open doors.

"Their guns are out, that's promising," said Ralph.

Indeed, the police harangued someone inside the tall, filthy apartment building to give themselves up.

"Oooooh, yeah." Albert rubbed his hands together. "Gonna get some! Get some tonight!"

"Would you shut up? I hate that song. And stop dancing, you're shaking the ground. Someone will notice."

"Bah." Albert considered a comment about exactly which of them was making the ground shake, but didn't want the distraction. "This is taking too long. Let's just go in and get him."

"Agreed. We've only been here half a day and I already hate this place."

Too irritated for stealth, they walked through the building's front door. Following the shouting, they found their target on the third floor, his door barricaded.

"Let's go on three." Ralph stepped back to his ideal

kicking range. "One … Two …"

"Wait, on three, or 'one, two, three,' then go?"

"Not this crap again." Ralph booted the door in, leaping into a tumble and extending his forearm knives as he landed in a crouch. He searched the room before looking at Albert. "Where is he?"

Albert pointed to the bedroom door, also closed. Waving Ralph away, he crept across the room and put his ear against the thin, wooden barrier. "Unbelievable. He's talking to the cops on the phone right now. The whole thing's a big misunderstanding." Albert paused to listen. "Apparently he told a joke?" He stood straight up, his head brushing the ceiling. "I'm so sick of this crap. There's no one here worth killing! You know what?" He punched a button on his forearm computer, and the cannon on his shoulder came to life. "To hell with the rules, I'm killing something, now."

A tussle ensued as Ralph held Albert in a bear hug and talked him down. The bedroom door opened, and a confused man exited, phone still stuck to his ear.

"Hello?" he said. "Who's there? I already apologized and said I was coming down to surrender to your diversity officer. It's very hurtful that you'd do violence to my front door like that."

The hunters stared at the man, jaws agape.

"Let me go," said Albert, a dangerous serenity obliging Ralph to comply.

An easy jog brought them back to the shuttle that evening. Cal waited at the bottom of the ramp, giddiness threatening to burst from his chest.

"So how'd it go?" He fought hard to contain his snickers, with some success.

"This place sucks," said Albert. "We should nuke the entire site from orbit."

"You knew, didn't you?" shouted Ralph, once he'd stopped wheezing. "That's why you volunteered to watch the ship." He stepped toward Cal, fists balled.

Cal threw his hands out in a placating gesture as the laughter dam broke. "Actually it's worse." He nodded at the ramp over his shoulder.

"Surprise!" A group of hunters sprang from the bushes surrounding them.

A grinning celebrity walked down the ramp, holding a camera on his shoulder. "You just got punked!"

Critical Magic

"Racism."

I looked up from my magic eight ball to see my friend's face crumble at the answer. "I'm so sorry."

She'd asked, on a whim, what her greatest flaw was. I tried to warn her that this thing was no joke, but she wouldn't listen.

"It's okay." She sniffled. "I have a lot of work to do. I think I'll go now." She shuffled a bit, staring at her feet. The silence stretched to awkwardness, and she left with nary a word.

A week passed, and my roommate returned from holiday vacation, full of solstice cheer. Eventually I tired of the cultural trauma she inflicted by tossing the C-word around like a drunken sailor, and chastised her insensitivity.

"What's your problem?" she demanded.

"It's not my problem we need to discuss," I brandished my enchanted ball and she blanched, word having reached her of its prophetic prowess. Holding her gaze I gave it a theatrical shake. "You're problem is …" She leaned forward, straining to see the outcome. "Racism."

Crushed. She was crushed, and I was free of her colonizer prattling.

Soon I courted many a visitor, all sheepishly requesting use of my divination talents. The majority

I saw fit to deny. Using the power drained me, almost as if each answer could only be coaxed forth by chipping away at my soul. I wasn't sure how much I could afford to sacrifice, and as the word "Faustian" echoed in my head, I realized I might well have damned myself.

It had begun as a whisper.

Justice.

At first I dismissed it as a simple manifestation of my focus on improving humanity, but a week later, I heard it again.

Juuuuustice.

Cutting through the library at the time, I peered at the stacks surrounding me. There were several nerds, whiling away at their books, but none seemed to notice me. I shrugged it off, hurried to secure my tacos, and endeavored to take the long route next time.

The next morning, before dawn could rescue my innocence, I was jarred from slumber by the gnawing hymn.

Justice!

With my roommate still asleep, I opened myself to the sensation I wasn't alone.

"Justice," I whispered to the dark.

You crave justice.

"Yes," I whispered, no longer afraid.

Look at my balls ...

"Oh come on," I said. My roommate stirred.

Sorry, couldn't resist.

I frowned, and was about to rebuke whatever juvenile prankster had disturbed me, when a prickling in my right shoulder caused me to turn my head. By the faint glow of the moon, I saw it. The magic eight ball. I dropped my voice again. "What do I do?"

Shake the baaaaaall. Truths shrouded by the sinister machinations of your oppressors will be revealed.

Confused if the voice meant men or white people, my reluctant hands grasped the sorcerous tool. Immediately, a foreign sensation flooded me, and I reflexively checked my inner thighs to see if I'd left my TENS unit on overnight again. I hadn't. And yet, the foreboding I anticipated was forestalled by the need to shake the voice's ball.

I shook. Slowly at first, but within the first shakes, an undeniable righteousness flowed from the ball into my hands. I shook harder. A serenity descended, and I knew it was time. I would soon learn the single most fundamental truth. What bound everything together. From the bacteria ravaging my unbrushed teeth, to the primordial matter that existed in the trillionths of a second before the Big Bang, I was about to grasp the thread that connected all life, everywhere.

Racism.

That was the moment. My life, my purpose, everything was revealed. It was in that moment, the moment of revelation from beyond, that I swore the oath.

The Hunt for Green October

"Down periscope!" Captain DiAngels had seen enough, it was time to act. "Take us to depth two hundred, bearing ninety degrees." *Green October*, The New York Times' latest attack submarine, dropped like a statue of Abraham Lincoln.

Her first officer, Commander Kotes, knew enough about the precarious nature of their mission to be alarmed. He approached with a low voice, unwilling to question her in front of the bridge crew. "Captain, there must be another way."

DiAngels placed a hand on Kotes' shoulder. "I wish there was." She turned to bellow at the others. "Load tubes one and two."

"Contact!" shouted Lieutenant Jones on sonar. "Bearing one-nine-zero."

"Cut engines, hard to port, drop to five hundred meters," said DiAngels. "Jesus, that's right behind us. How'd that son of a bitch out maneuver us so fast?"

A fresh noise cut through the bridge speakers before Kotes could answer.

"Torpedo in the water! It's ..." the sonar officer focused on the sound. "It's a racist-class torpedo, Captain. It's locked on us."

"Fire countermeasures, full speed, hard to starboard. I want tubes three and four loaded with racists. Fire the second you have a lock."

"Yes sir," said the weapons officer, repeating the instructions into his headset. Ten anxious seconds passed. They could hear the racist-class torpedo edging closer. "Firing solution. Fire, fire, fire." He turned to the Captain. "Tubes three and four fired, Ma'am."

For a tense minute, both boats weaved in an attempt to break the racist lock.

"A miss, Captain," yelled Jones. "Both ours missed. Theirs is following the new countermeasures, but it's going to be close. Impact in ten …" he counted them down to one, and the submarine shook from the nearby explosion. "Alarms in engine one, Captain, that hurt us."

Captain DiAngels was *pissed*. "Enough playing around. Tubes three and four, I want a sexist- and a transphobe-class torpedo. Fire when locked."

"Another fish in the water. Racist-class again," said the sonar officer.

DiAngels laughed. "Rookie." She raised her voice. "Deploy Anti-Racist smokescreen. Hard to port, come to depth one hundred. Where are my torpedoes, gentlemen?"

"Acquiring target and … fire three, fire four. Fish away, Captain."

Green October rose, trailing a chaotic churn of noise, smoke, and confusion as the Anti-Racist smokescreen hid their intentions from all but those clever enough to look at what they were doing.

"Racism detonated harmlessly against our

smokescreen, Ma'am," said Jones. "Contact deploying anti-sexist countermeasures." The bridge speakers blared a woman's voice decrying the torpedo as scurrilous and false. "A miss. Transphobe still locked and closing." Jones spun his chair to face DiAngels and Kotes. "I don't think he saw that coming."

The torpedo impacted with the target's hull, a thunderous boom echoing over the speakers. Captain DiAngels let her crew cheer for a few seconds before calling for quiet. She knew her adversary. He was crippled, but his double hull meant he was still alive, and dangerous. Several pings sounded against *Green October*. Morse code.

S-O-S

"Take us to periscope depth, nice and slow. I want two ableist-class fish loaded in tubes three and four. If he blinks, fire." She granted herself permission to smile as they parked on the surface, and the first crackle of the short-range radio sounded across the bridge.

"I'm sorry for the pain I have caused," said the voice. "I have so much to learn. I understand that my actions have caused unnecessary pain and suffering, and will be taking some time away to meditate on the harm I've caused …"

DiAngels laughed and signaled Jones to cut the speakers. She didn't need to hear the rest. She was about to get paid.

Life Support

I wasn't going to lose this one.

I'd lost so many patients in the past, you'd think I'd have grown a second skin. And maybe I had, but if I let this one die, I knew it would change everything.

"Clear!" I shouted. The other doctors lifted their hands, and raw voltage seared through his body.

"We have a pulse!" said a nurse, relieving me of the defibrillator. "It's weak. We're losing him."

We had to stop the bleeding. His heart was leaking blood faster than we could mainline it into his vein.

"Clamps." I thrust an empty palm toward the cart beside me, and a nurse filled it. "Lift, dammit," I snarled at my fellow MDs. I leaned in closer and held my breath. *There.* A minute tear. I clamped it, and the leak slowed. The patient stabilized.

"Needle." I started to sew, aware the clamps could slip at any moment. God-like serenity flowed through me as I closed the gap. A minute passed. Two. Mere seconds to me.

I exhaled and leaned back to examine my work. It held. Exhaustion assaulted me, and I stumbled a step. A nurse was beside me immediately, steadying me. I assured him I was fine, and allowed someone else to verify the stitches.

We observed the patient for half an hour before

leaving the Operating Room. By then we were all equally spent, and dreading the predictable demonstrations awaiting us. The shouting, the anger, the disbelief.

"How could you save such a monster?"
"Don't you know what he's done?"
"For the love of God, just let him die."
"How can you live with yourself?"

We'd heard it all, and knew we'd hear it again. So short sighted. They didn't grasp the principles at stake, the bigger picture. What we did that morning would echo through universities for decades.

For the greater good, he had to survive.

Ascendancy

Looking back, I can't pinpoint the moment it started. The surge, the siphoning of life energy from those around me.

My instinct, as the power coursed through my hands, was panic. What began as a light tingling rapidly intensified, becoming painful until I willed its diffusion amongst my limbs. In those first, surreal moments, I recall lifting my right hand and examining it with new eyes. My hand balled into a fist of its own accord, and the potential energy I felt inside it terrified me.

I scrutinized my surroundings with all the subtlety a nineteen year old at an anti-Nazi rally could muster, and thanked mother Gaia for the bedlam that camouflaged me. The same mental agility that innervated my moral indignation allowed me to adapt to my new power in moments, my sole fear being the indiscriminate nature of its siphoning.

But *was* it indiscriminate?

With great power comes great responsibility.

The sages of antiquity ejaculated their wisdom upon me. I formed a plan to test my powers. First the accumulation, then their application, finally, their limits. At a glance, I found my first subject. Sarah, a fellow sophomore, chanted beside me, oblivious to fate's thread. I focused on her, drawing her energy toward me. Nothing happened. She was pretty hot, so rather than further risk her safety, I shifted to an unappealing stranger on my opposite flank.

Nothing. I doubled my efforts.

Still nothing.

As my momentum sagged, I stumbled upon a breakthrough. Casually, my mind elsewhere, I flung the word 'racist' at the college president. Never in my long years inhabiting this shell of flesh had I witnessed an impact such as that from my denunciation. The man, middle aged before I spoke, flinched as if the waves sent hurtling by my word of power were justice made manifest. Then, before I could grasp my power, it happened.

"I'm sorry."

Two words, so reflexively offered as to be meaningless. Yet, they weren't. The now-familiar tingling reignited my extremities. The energy I had expended in my assault was recovered.

"Racist!" I shouted again. Time dilated as the force of my accusation engulfed the foolish administrator. He staggered backwards. More cries rang true, the crowd pressed forward.

"Please," he yelled. "I'm very sorry."

He aged, feeding my strength.

"The administration recognizes the racism inherent in our words and actions."

My body swelled with the life force of this pitiful man.

"We promise to give serious consideration to your

list of demands."

I flung my head back in ecstasy. "No!" I cried, the spectral quality of my voice commanding the president's obeisance. "You will grant them now. *All of them.*"

Without having read our demands, I understood this fool would acquiesce. It was all a mortal could do in the face of unbridled moral supremacy. In the face of my ascendancy.

The Eagle, the Bear, and the Dragon

An eagle and a bear sat discussing their various aches and pains.

"I am quite worried," said the eagle. "This feels serious."

"Bah." The bear waved a mighty paw. "You say that all the time. To be alive is to fight many sicknesses at once."

"This feels serious," the eagle repeated. "Like the sickness is attacking the parts of me that exist to fight other sicknesses."

"I still think you are fine. Remember when you were born? You had two terrible viruses. But you lived."

The eagle grew sad, thinking of his infancy. Those two viruses had left him permanently stained. "This is definitely not as bad as those. But this sickness wants to change me, I know that much."

"Maybe you *should* change," hissed the dragon hiding in the shadows.

"Yes, change is often a good thing," agreed the bear.

The eagle frowned at the dragon. "Hush you, you think of no one but yourself. You hide your diseases, and celebrate them in others, hoping they grow weak enough for you to devour."

The dragon hissed and snapped in the eagle's direction, but it wasn't big enough to attack. Yet. The bear watched with a smirk, sipping a pungent drink.

"Life is change," said the eagle. "I must grow new feathers to replace the old. But this sickness eats away at my very innards. If it does not subside, I will be more crippled than changed."

The dragon loosed a sinister chuckle.

The bear shrugged. "I have never been happy, why should I care if you are."

"Because dragons like to eat bears too."

The bear shrugged again.

The eagle studied the bear. "You do not know what I will change into," it finally said. "This sickness is so very aggressive, and does not care if it destroys me entirely, only that it gets its own way. There is no plan for what follows, and no reason to believe that what follows will be better. For any of us."

The bear and the dragon thought about what the eagle said, and realized it was true. But as the eagle's sickness was destroying body parts neither of them had, they were happy to watch it die.

Jeffrey's Pimple

Jeffrey had a pimple. It was right on his nose, and it shone like a lantern in the night.

It was a stubborn pimple, and though Jeffrey attacked it each morning, it seemed to possess a supernatural resilience. But the pimple eventually gave ground, dimming over time. Jeffrey was grateful.

Then, as the pimple commanded less of his attention, Jeffrey began noticing other pimples. He attended to those as well.

One day, Jeffrey's mother interrupted him as he gazed at a pool of still water.

"What are you doing? There's work to be done," she said.

"I'm looking for pimples," he replied.

His mother thought him foolish, but was too busy with the other children to discipline him. Thus he lay there, hunting for blemishes. And blemishes he found, for no face was ever perfect, not even for a moment.

But Jeffrey quickly dealt with the obvious pimples, and, enjoying the hunt, was loathe to stop. Besides, if he finished looking for pimples, his mother would put him to work on far more difficult tasks. So he found smaller and smaller blemishes.

Absorbed as he was in his crusade, Jeffrey forgot to

eat. As he stared at his reflection, pecking incessantly at his skin, he grew weaker. Soon Jeffrey was so weak, it was all he could do to gouge the tiniest blemish from his face, which by then was riddled with scabs. One day, he lacked the strength even for that, and realized his predicament. He sought to call his mother, that she might help, but even his voice failed him.

Eventually, Jeffrey's mother returned, seeking her errant child. She stopped where he lay, never imagining the long, narrow lump of grass she stood upon was her sweet, foolish boy. Sometimes, if you listen, deeeeeep in the forest, you can hear a woman's voice calling his name.

Jeffrey's Pimple - Alternate Ending

Jeffrey had a pimple. It was right on his nose, and it shone like a lantern in the night.

It was a stubborn pimple, and though Jeffrey attacked it each morning, it seemed to possess a supernatural resilience. But the pimple eventually gave ground, dimming over time. Jeffrey was grateful.

Then, as the pimple commanded less of his attention, Jeffrey began noticing other pimples. He attended to those as well.

One day, Jeffrey's mother interrupted him as he gazed at a pool of still water.

"What are you doing? There's work to be done," she said.

"I'm looking for pimples," he replied.

"Let me see." Jeffrey's mother knelt beside him and examined him. "Every inch of every face will always have flaws. Your task is to improve the ones you can, not obsessively gouge away until nothing is left." She turned him to and fro. "There's nothing wrong with your face, young man. I've needed your help for days, yet here you sit."

"How can you say there's nothing wrong with my face, mother? Look at this!" He pointed to a spot on his cheek.

His mother leaned in close. "Goodness me, are you pecking at that tiny thing?"

"It's a blemish, mother. I *must* fix it."

"A blemish indeed, but your pecking isn't fixing it, it's inflaming it. Why, look at the scabs you've created around it!"

"That was not my doing, mother. Educate yourself."

A quick wallop upside the boy's head ended the discussion, and he helped his mother for the rest of the day. But the next morning he was missing. His mother stomped directly to the pool of water, again finding the boy staring at his reflection, disgust evident on his features.

"Get yourself away from that reflection this instant, young man," she said, hands on hips.

"Why? What don't you want me to see? What are you hiding?" As he spoke, the boy sat up, and looked at his mother.

With a shriek, she rushed forward and cradled his head. "Oh my sweet, sweet, foolish child."

Dear Johns

I'm sorry to end it like this, but I can't do this anymore.

I know, writing a letter is cliché. Spineless even, you could argue. But I'm not sure how else I'd have done it.

The sad reality is we're not meant to be. I wish I could offer the standard "we've drifted apart," rationale, but it's you. You've changed.

When we met, you were fun. You were heavy when life required it, but you didn't take everything so serious. So personal. At this point, I never know what's going to set you off.

I should probably stop here, but I'm going to risk hurting you, angering you, because for some stupid reason I still care about you and want you to succeed. To be happy. To stop stewing in the bitterness that makes you lash out in every direction. So please, promise me you'll read until the end before reacting. Here goes nothing.

Not everything is about you.

Most people aren't thinking about you as much as you are. They're good people if you'd just give them a chance! The number of people who hate you, fear you, wish you harm, is orders of magnitude smaller than you imagine. Most people are struggling the same as you are, just making it through each week. They have kids, rent, a car insurance bill they forgot to pay. They're worried about being laid off, or whether their health insurance will cover them if, God forbid, they get cancer. The amount of animosity you're projecting into the world doesn't reflect any of that.

Your priorities are your own, and maybe they make sense for you. I don't think they do, but you're an adult, you get to make that choice for yourself. But you don't get to make it for me, and you don't get to judge me for not shifting my attention to whatever happens to be pissing you off that day.

And that's another problem - you're mad at something new every week, sometimes every day. I can't keep up! And when I tell you I'm drowning, you blame me. You blame me for not taking the world's problems as my own, when you won't even take responsibility for things directly under your control. How did *you* spend your day yesterday? It's tragic enough to be comical. In a decade.

With all that, I think I could stay if you didn't shut down around me whenever I tried to talk to you. Maybe anger is pain's shield, but I can't live with the constant recriminations. I can't live knowing that any time we disagree you're going to attack me, call me names, and change the subject to how terrible I am.

You're a bully. When we disagree, you run me over like a freight train, and walk away like you proved whatever point your knickers are twisted about that afternoon. You never stop to consider that maybe you're just more aggressive. That your points are garbage, but you scare people into submission. People aren't agreeing with you, they're hiding from you. Maybe that was something you had to do a long time ago when you were speaking truth to power. But now you *are* power, and it's terrifying.

I've already blabbered on too long, but I need to make one last point. There isn't anyone else. I'm not leaving you for "that other guy" (you know who I mean), I'm just leaving. You've caused so much damage, gone so far off the rails, that I need to be alone for awhile.

You'll always be in my heart, and in time I'll think back on you, my circle of leftist friends, with love and nostalgia.

Sincerely,
Tired Moderate

The Preview

This is a preview of the woke romance I'm currently writing. The carnality isn't gratuitous, but it's there. If that bugs you, well, stop reading here.

A white woman of perhaps forty, adorned in a 1920s flapper costume, seduced a white man of similar age. Smooth jazz floated softly among us, and she coyly pushed him into the room's lone, wooden chair. Circling him, she produced handcuffs, carefully locking her victim into place without ruffling his pinstripe suit.

"She's amazing," I whispered to Robert, unwilling to tear my gaze from her as I spoke.

"They," he said. "Both prefer 'they/them.'"

I apologized, half-heartedly, riveted as I was by their mesmerizing performance.

The man was locked loosely in place, with no sign of testing their bonds. The woman stood in front of them, facing the other direction and peering into a faux distance as if hunting for someone. With a quick tug, the feather boa slid from their neck, 'accidentally' falling to the ground. Feigning embarrassment, they slowly bent at the waist to retrieve it, casting a lascivious eye toward their victim.

They matched their gaze and raised them a crooked smile. Boa in hand, they twirled on their platform heels and stalked toward them. Now, their willpower cracking, they *did* strain against their bonds, their groin rising ever so slightly toward them.

With playful gravity, they wagged a finger at them. They eased back into the chair, and the dance began anew. Flipping the boa around their neck, they teased their way around them, brushing hips, fingers, and hair against every part of their body. After several tormentous turns, they sat on one of their legs, facing them. They began a slow, rhythmic grind, and I belatedly realized the music had shifted from smooth jazz to sensual electronica.

Their hands roamed freely, across their face, their neck. Using their boa like a snare, they yanked them into a long and forceful kiss, only to break it long before their prey was ready. They strained openly now, desperate to recapture their lips with theirs. They shoved them backwards and, with a heave, tore their dress shirt open before grabbing their throat to hold them in place for the kiss they craved.

Breaking free again, they kissed their neck, nipping at it, then moving to their lean chest. Their hands stayed ahead of their mouth until they reached their groin, where they avoided their manhood. The remains of their admirable self control nearly crumbled when they unzipped their pants and gripped them. Kneeling now, they looked up at them and pressed a finger to their lips. Satisfied, they gave their member a teasing kiss. Then, a teasing lick. An exquisite torture followed, until they abruptly stood and straddled their lap.

They ground their center against there's, repeating until I, just watching, felt a frantic need to complete the act. With a practiced movement, they used one hand to slide their panties aside, and the other to guide them inside them.

Their moan liberated my breath, which I had no memory of holding. They raised themself slowly, lowering themself even slower. Eyes locked onto theirs, daring them to assert themself, they raised themself again, this time slamming their body on to theirs. Something seemed to break inside of them, and they rode them with a dangerously contagious frenzy.

The woman bit into their neck as they returned to a grinding motion. This proved too much, and, with a shout, the man shuddered in release. They continued grinding as they too built to climax. Stopping, they leaned back to use their hand on themself, finally screaming themself to completion.

I don't know how long they sat on their lap as they gently nuzzled. Eventually Robert led me again by the arm, introducing me to at least a dozen partygoers. I didn't remember any of it. The haze of what I'd witnessed was impenetrable. What I remember is expecting Robert to tear my dress off me, rip my panties apart, and ravish me, and for me to let him. But he didn't. Instead he was the perfect gentleman, delivering me, grievously unravished, to my parent's door.

The Author

Trigger warning! Tired Moderate is not really my name.

Comedy mocks the absurd.

Other works of mine include:
- Woke Fragility: Bringing Moderates to Heel
- The Little Book of Woke Jokes

If you enjoyed this, please take a minute to leave a review on Amazon, Goodreads, or any other site you use. The almighty algorithms use the number of reviews to determine which books to recommend.

Printed in Great Britain
by Amazon